ZO...
NEMESIS™

UNAUTHORIZED
SECRETS & SOLUTIONS

NOW AVAILABLE FROM PRIMA

Computer Game Books

How to Order:
For information on quantity discounts contact the publisher: Prima Publishing, P.O. Box 1260BK, Rocklin, CA 95677-1260; (916) 632-4400. On your letterhead include information concerning the intended use of the books and the number of books you wish to purchase. For individual orders, turn to the back of the book for more information.

ZORK
NEMESIS™

UNAUTHORIZED
SECRETS & SOLUTIONS

RICK BARBA

PRIMA PUBLISHING

Project Editor: Dallas Middaugh

ISBN: 0-7615-0711-6
Library of Congress Catalog Card Number: 96-68005

Printed in the United States of America
96 97 98 99 DD 10 9 8 7 6 5 4 3 2 1

CONTENTS

ACKNOWLEDGMENTS

Let's see, who to acknowledge? OK, I acknowledge myself. Can I do that? This is an unauthorized book, so I got no help from anybody in my navigation of *Zork Nemesis*. Well, there was some guy named "Anji," an early conqueror who posted good hints on the AOL message boards. Thanks, man. Whoever you are. And thanks to my family for tossing occasional food packets into the office as I dropped off the radar screen of life.

Thanks also to my editors—Dallas Middaugh for his expert stewardship of a project which proceeded at superluminal speed, and Juliana Aldous for snagging the very first copy of Zork Nemesis to fall off the truck, I think. Thanks to Marian Hartsough for another elegant book design. Thanks to Prima—Ben, Roger, Juliana, Brett, Debbie, Nancy, all those guys—for being so darn swell. And what the hell. I'd like to thank every person in Boulder, Colorado, for constituting such a rocking town in which to live.

I'm in a pretty good mood today.

Rick Barba
Boulder, CO
April 10, 1996

INTRODUCTION

elcome to your infallible guide to *Zork Nemesis*. This book offers you the best step-by-step solution path through the game, as well as various maps to help you navigate its five locations. You also get an added bonus—a review and detailed walk-through for *Return to Zork*, the award-winning and highly entertaining predecessor to *Zork Nemesis*.

Note that this is an "unauthorized" strategy guide. This means I didn't have *Zork Nemesis* handed to me on a silver platter (along with *croissants* and such) by Activision. I had to approach *Zork Nemesis* exactly as you did. I bought it when it came out. I played it for hours, without help. I got frustrated in the same places you did. And I powered through the game—gamer style—all by myself. (Well, OK . . . I checked out a few message boards on the Internet. But that's what gamers do.)

The only difference between me and you is that playing games is my job. So I got to spend an entire week of 12 to 14-hour days scouring The Forbidden Lands, exploring every nook and cranny while cobbling together a comprehensive walk-through—a week of almost pure Zork, interrupted only by sleep, *Seinfeld*, and occasional food intake.

Of course, most of you don't have that luxury. That's why you bought this book.

ZORK: THE LEGEND CONTINUES

Zork Nemesis is the latest in a venerable series of games set in the empire of Zork. Adventure game lovers, young and old, have made a cult of worshipping the classic Infocom text adventures—*Zork I, Zork II, Zork III, Beyond Zork, Zork Zero*. Indeed, if you're an adventure gamer and you've never been Zorked, you're missing a real treat. Unlike many current games, the old Infocom text-only adventures featured clean, clever writing. They *had* to, since there were no multimedia pyrotechnics to lay a smoke-screen over lame storytelling in those days.

So, Zork is back. And yes, that's good news. *Zork Nemesis* is not only a worthy successor to the Zork throne, it is one of the most impressive games I've ever seen in *any* genre. The story, the acting, the art, the sound and music, the technology engine—all of it is stunning, even miraculous. Without hesitation, I rank *Zork Nemesis* right up in the highest echelon of graphic adventure gaming, alongside such titles as *Myst, Under a Killing Moon*, and all those Sierra and LucasArts classics.

Fortunately for certain writers of strategy guides, *Zork Nemesis* is also one of the most diabolically difficult adventure games ever designed. Look, I'm a pretty seasoned adventure game player— again, it's part of my job. (Grueling work, yes, but I make millions, so don't feel sorry for me.) I hack through most games in a couple of days. But *Zork Nemesis* was a bear. It's immense. It offers up a vast, complex, and utterly absorbing game world. For most casual gamers, an unaided sojourn through The Forbidden Lands could take weeks. Months, even.

That's fine, if you can handle frustration. If not—if you're like me, impatient to see the story unfold, and prone to punch things when you get stuck—then you bought the right book. Either way, it's worth it. *Zork Nemesis* is a great game.

HOW TO USE THIS BOOK

Yes, this is a cheat book. It gives you a step-by-step, no-nonsense solution path through *Zork Nemesis*. So be warned. I don't try to protect you from yourself. No coy hints, no upside-down printing—just answers. If you don't have the willpower to stop reading after you've found the particular information you need, I suggest you seek some form of therapy.

When you're stuck somewhere in the game, simply go to the chapter for that location—Temple, Monastery, Conservatory, Castle, or Asylum—and check the map. You might find a useful clue. Or not. You might need to explore the chapter itself. If so, start from the beginning of the chapter and go forward until you find the heading for the room that has you stumped. (This way you won't stumble onto an answer for a later visit to the same room.)

A QUICK NOTE ABOUT MAPS

OK, I admit it, I'm not a cartographer. So don't get all Zorked out when you notice that my maps aren't drawn *precisely* to scale. In this game, that's not important. All you need to know is where the rooms are, where the doors are, and where certain important items are located. My maps include everything you need in order to navigate successfully through the five locations in the game.

Also note: Just because you see a door on the map doesn't mean you can *open* it. Many doors are locked permanently, or they can be opened only from the other side. When you can't open a door, just move on. Don't obsess over it. And tell me, when did "obsess" become a verb? I need to know, man. I need to know *now*.

GETTING STARTED

This book assumes that you've already read the manual that comes with *Zork Nemesis* and that you've already mastered the game's incredibly easy-to-use interface. It also assumes that you read Archive File #A-NEM/FOBILA, the informative booklet that comes with the game. If you haven't read these documents, do so now. (I'll wait right here until you get back.)

OK, good. That's all you need to know to get started.

But you expect more from me. I can see that. So here's the setup. Your immediate task is to retrace the path of Agent Karlok Bivotar in his search for four missing people, all apparently abducted by the mysterious Nemesis. These four are alchemists of note, and, as you see in their files from the Bureau of Missing Citizens, all four were last seen heading toward the Temple of Agrippa in the Desert River Province.

The four missing citizens are General Thaddeus Kaine, Liege of Castle Irondune, Desert River Province; Madame Sophia Hamilton, Headmistress of the Frigid River Branch Conservatory, Desert River Province; Bishop Francois Malveaux, Bishop of Zork, Steppinthrax Zorkastrian Monastery, Aragain Province; and Doctor Erasmus Sartorius, Chief of Staff, Gray Mountains Asylum, Gray Mountain Province.

Bivotar's journal and other effects also reveal that you must complete two other tasks: First, explore the Forbidden Lands and seek confirmation of a mind-altering "curse" said to afflict these regions. Second, find and document any use of unauthorized magic in the realm. Bivotar suspects that the Nemesis itself, whoever he is, is wielding black magic arts for his own dark purposes, whatever they may be.

THE OPENING

The introductory movie opens with the disturbing image of some long-haired guy ramming a knife into himself. After a nice close-up of a gaping stab wound, we hear a woman's voice. She speaks of murder, of lost love, and a curse that has unraveled the future. Then she says, "Only the four lost elements will bring the world back into balance."

And thus the adventure begins.

CHAPTER ONE

TEMPLE OF AGRIPPA

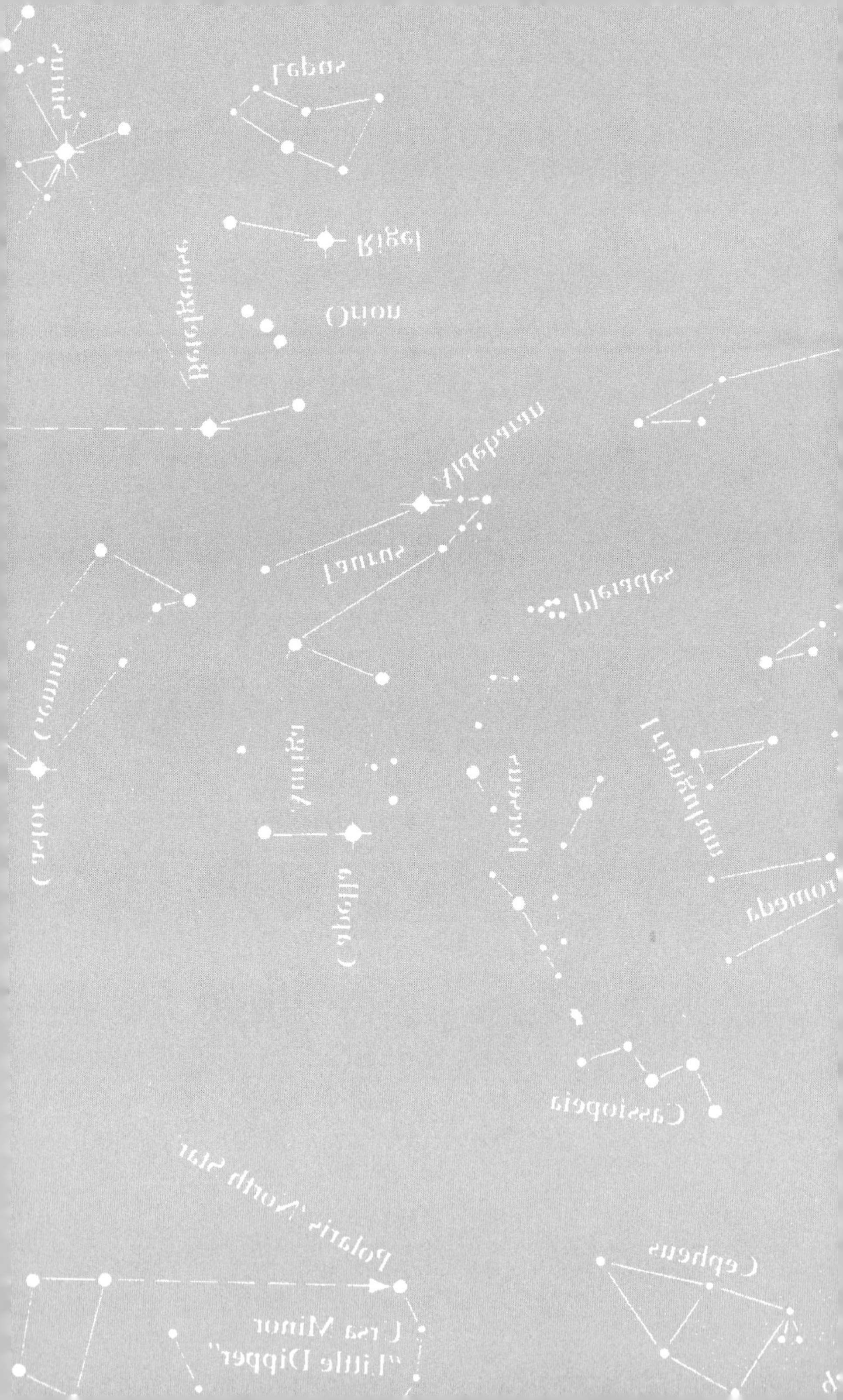

Little Dipper

Polaris, the
North Star

Cepheus

Cassiopeia

Perseus

Triangulum

Pleiades

Auriga

Capella

Taurus

Aldebaran

Gemini (Castor)

Orion

Betelgeuse

Rigel

Lepus

Sirius

s the game begins, you find yourself in the courtyard of the Temple of the Ancients, which you know to be the lair of the Nemesis himself. Nice place to start, eh? Behind you is a chained gate that you cannot open. So forget about escape, unless you choose the cowardly Ctrl-Alt-Delete route. Ahead of you rises a stairway that leads to an antechamber of the Temple.

COURTYARD

- Go forward up the stairs.
- When you reach the sun engraving on the wall, turn right and go forward.
- Turn left and go forward.
- Turn left and enter the antechamber through the open door.

ANTECHAMBER

- Cross the room to the burning candle.
- Click on the candle to trigger the appearance of a ghostly apparition. It approaches you, asks for help, then says, "They're in the Temple." When the apparition disappears, step back.
- Turn right and approach the crypt.
- Click on the crypt. After the violin plays, click on the crypt again to look inside.
- Click on the note for a close-up. Yikes! Click to put the note back.
- Back away from the crypt, and turn around to face the door.
- Go forward twice to exit the room.
- Work your way around the outside of the antechamber until you can cross the courtyard to the ornate door.

SUN/MOON DOOR

- Look up, then click on the sign and read it. Some might call it a clue. I call it a gift.

4

❦ Back away from the sign and click on the left door knocker.

❦ In the close-up, click and hold on to the bottom of the knocker (a moon), and then drag it up onto the sun at the top.

INNER HALL

❦ After the door opens, go forward and listen to the friendly voice of your local Nemesis.

❦ Turn right and enter the Library through the open door.

LIBRARY

❦ Turn left and go forward.

❦ Turn left and click on each of the books on the near shelf. From right to left, they are:

Excerpt from *My Best Excesses*

By Lord Dimwit Flathead

You'll find nothing of value in this book, unless you value goofy neo-Swiftian satire.

Alchemy of Pure Love

By C. Barajas

You can explore one page of this text. In it, the author proclaims "pure love" as the Fifth Element—the Quintessence that you seek. The passage also posits the sun and moon as "two Magicall Principles"—the first masculine, the other feminine. A note scrawled on the right facing page reads: "Explore this further in lab."

The Best of The New Zorker

Here you find an excerpt which mentions the unrest and dark events that plague the Forbidden Lands. Are they really cursed? Rhetorical question, of course. The article also mentions the disappearance of General Kaine.

Interview with a Grue

By Andrew Zilber

A flattering portrait of a Grue in confinement. No, the non-picture isn't a graphic glitch. Zork fans know that a Grue's "natural habitat" is pitch black darkness, ha ha ha.

Astronomy for a New Age: The Brogmoid Fallacy, Or Why the Earth Is Not Flat After All

By Dr. Curl Zaygan, PhZ

Now here's a helpful tome. Note first the illustrations of the planets on the left-hand page. Hey . . . aren't those the names of the missing alchemists? Malveaux on Saturnax, Kaine on Murz, Sartorius on Juperon, Sophia on Venus-nv. Serious clue here. Note also the picture of the planetarium on the next page, and the scribbled note.

Untitled

This journal is most disturbing. Especially the "ripped their throats out" thing. This Nemesis guy is not happy. The sketch on the right-hand page is important, but don't copy it down. You'll find it on page 13 of the game manual as well as on the last page of the Bivotar journal. Turn the page to learn that the four elements (Earth, Air, Fire, Water) are hidden in the Temple.

℄ OK, enough book browsing. Turn right and exit through that doorway in the corner of the library.

FOUNTAIN ATRIUM

℘ Turn left and go forward twice to reach the end of the walkway.

℘ Ignore the Nemesis threat. Turn left and enter the lab.

LABORATORY

℘ Just inside the door, turn right until you see the notebook leaning against the box.

℘ Open the notebook and read the pages.

Here you learn that the Nemesis has linked each alchemist with their respective signs:

> Malveaux – fire
>
> Sartorius – air
>
> Kaine – earth
>
> Sophia – water

Of course, if you read Bivotar's journal, you already knew these elemental associations. But since most sentient beings don't read in-box documentation, this is probably helpful information. Turn the page to learn that the Nemesis has hidden their alchemical elements in the Temple, guarding each with elaborate security devices.

℘ After exiting the journal, swivel to the right (past the door) and go forward.

℘ Turn left to face the wall tapestry. Click on it to hear . . . faint violin music? Isn't that the same haunting melody played by that floating violin in the antechamber crypt?

℘ Turn left and go forward.

- Turn left and go forward.
- Click on the photos on the desk to uncover the portrait of the girl playing a violin. Click on it again for a close-up. Do you see a violin motif developing here?
- Exit the close-up, turn left, and go forward.
- Turn right and go forward.
- Turn left and look down at the broken elemental symbols. Click on them for a light show, if you want. Exit the close-up.
- Turn 180 degrees and look down at the etching of the mandala. Note that Malveaux's name is scribbled at the top. Exit the close-up.
- Turn left and go towards the ladder.
- Climb the ladder.
- Turn right and examine the notebook.

Note the four drawings. The first depicts a man in a lab coat—a doctor, perhaps? He works at some sort of tube contraption. The second shows a man in a uniform—a soldier, maybe? He sits near a mining car full of dirt. The third drawing is of a hooded man—a monk, do you think? This fellow holds a lighted candle. The fourth and final drawing depicts a woman gazing into a pool of water. You don't suppose she's a headmistress at a local conservatory of music, do you?

- Climb back down the ladder, turn slightly left, then go forward into the back room.
- Click on each of the six talking disks. What a pleasant guy this Nemesis seems to be. Gosh, I can't wait to meet him.
- Turn slightly right and examine the scroll. Be sure to jot down the "correspondences" (and their symbols) listed

here. Then click on the scroll until you've read the entire manuscript.

This remarkable scroll speaks of alchemy, the art of extracting "perfect" essences from common materials. It speaks also of the Fifth Element, the secret "Quintessence" that offers great power to its possessor.

- Exit the Nemesis laboratory and go straight to the end of the walkway.
- Turn right and go forward once to get halfway down the walkway.
- Turn left and enter the corridor.

"VENUS" CORRIDOR

Go straight ahead into the main hall.

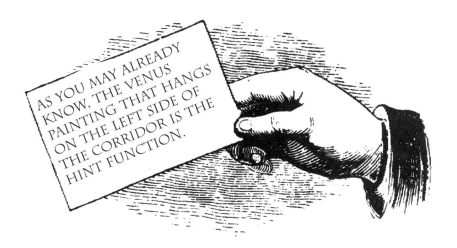

AS YOU MAY ALREADY KNOW, THE VENUS PAINTING THAT HANGS ON THE LEFT SIDE OF THE CORRIDOR IS THE HINT FUNCTION.

TEMPLE OF AGRIPPA

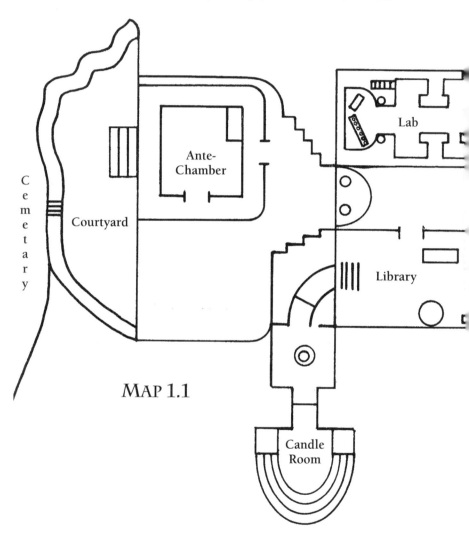

Lab

Cemetary

Ante-Chamber

Courtyard

Library

MAP 1.1

Candle Room

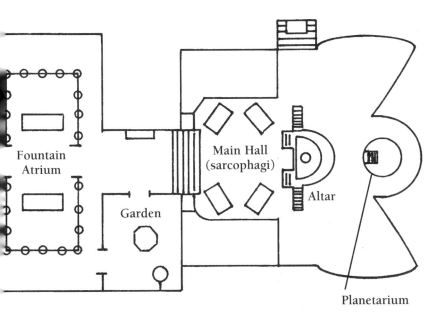

Fountain
Atrium

Main Hall
(sarcophagi)

Altar

Garden

Planetarium

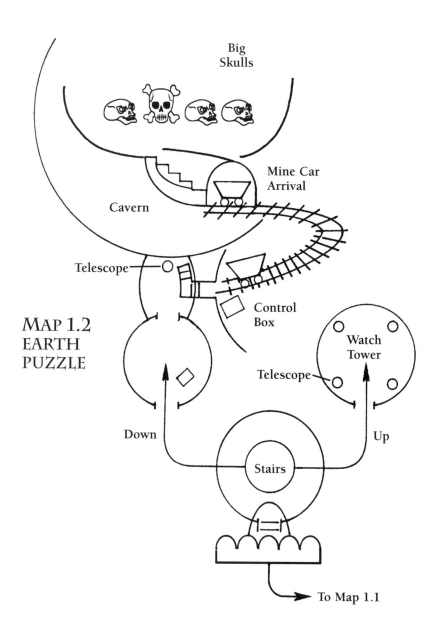

Big
Skulls

Mine Car
Arrival

Cavern

Telescope

MAP 1.2
EARTH
PUZZLE

Control
Box

Watch
Tower

Telescope

Down

Up

Stairs

To Map 1.1

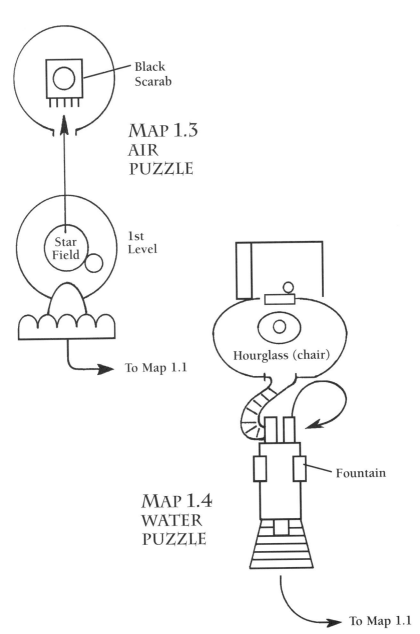

Black
Scarab

MAP 1.3
AIR
PUZZLE

Star
Field

1st
Level

To Map 1.1

Hourglass (chair)

Fountain

MAP 1.4
WATER
PUZZLE

To Map 1.1

MAIN HALL (SARCOPHAGI)

❧ Go to each of the four sarcophagi. At each one, brace your-self for some seriously hokey acting, then click twice on the "body" sealed within to get it talking.

You learn that these are the four missing alchemists—Sartorius, Malveaux, Kaine, and Sophia. You also discover what element each one requires. You know from clues in the lab that the Nemesis has hidden the four elements throughout the Temple. Your job now is to find these elements and bring them back to the entombed alchemists.

If you haven't figured out the corresponding signs for each alchemist yet, click on the masked skull above each person on the front of his/her sarcophagus.

❧ At the far end of the room is a raised platform with a circular altar. If you approach the altar, you see that it is engraved with the four triangles and four astrological symbols of the alchemists. You can't do anything here yet, but note it for later.

❧ Exit the main hall into the Venus corridor and turn left.

❧ Go straight ahead through the doorway into the garden.

Now you're ready to find the four elements. First, let's take a crack at the Fire Elemental puzzle.

FIRE ELEMENTAL PUZZLE

You need to bring the pure, alchemical essence of fire to Bishop Malveaux.

GARDEN

❧ Cross the garden to the sundial.

🜲 Click on the sundial for a close-up, and then take the rod from the top of the dial.

   🜲 Back away from the sundial, turn right, and go through the doorway into the fountain atrium.

   🜲 Go straight down the walkway into the library.

LIBRARY

   🜲 Cross the room and approach the sliding maps.

   🜲 Slide the first map to the left—i.e., click on its left side.

   🜲 Slide the second map to the right.

   🜲 Slide the third map to the right.

   🜲 Slide the fourth map to the left.

   🜲 Go forward into the newly-revealed hallway.

HALLWAY

   🜲 Turn left and approach the mandala at the end of the hall.

   🜲 Click and hold onto the head of the man in the mandala.

   🜲 Drag the mandala around until the man's head lines up with the triangle symbol at lower left.

   🜲 When the door opens, step forward into the next room.

SUNDIAL ROOM

   🜲 Approach the sundial.

   🜲 Put the rod (from the garden sundial) in the hole.

   🜲 Click and drag the rod to turn the sundial.

   🜲 Turn until the rod is at the upper left of the dial. The shadow of the rod must fall across the Saturnas symbol—which, of course, corresponds to Malveaux. A beam of light shoots from the mirror onto the door at the back of the room.

℃ After the door opens, go forward twice to enter the candle room.

CANDLE ROOM

℃ Just inside the door, turn right and take the mirror.

℃ Step into the center of the room.

℃ See the hooks that drop from the ceiling? Hang the mirror on the leftmost hook.

℃ Note the small candle with the blue flame reflected in the corner of the mirror. Turn right and click on it to get a close-up. (This may take a couple of tries.)

℃ In the close-up, click on the blue flame. This triggers a teleport back to that circular altar in the main hall.

MAIN HALL (SARCOPHAGI)

℃ Click on the flaming triangle on the dial.

℃ After the flame dies, go towards the now-glowing sarcophagus (second from left) of Bishop Malveaux.

Bishop Malveaux appears in the sun sculpture above the sarcophagus and thanks you. He speaks of his daughter Alexandria, slain by the Nemesis. He says he still hears her music. (That wouldn't be violin, would it?) Then he suggests there is a way to "bring her back."

EARTH ELEMENT PUZZLE

As you know from his journals of the Nemesis, the foul beast hid Kaine's elemental earth somewhere in the Temple. We know that Kaine's earth symbol is ♂. Locate the symbol on the map of the

Temple in the back of Bivotar's journal. The placement suggests that the element is hidden somewhere in the upper left corner of the main hall.

MAIN HALL (SARCOPHAGI)

- After Malveaux's message, head to the left side of the raised platform.
- In the back left corner of the vast hall, you find a door locked by a bar apparently held in place by skeleton fingers.
- Click on the finger at the far left to raise it. Note the symbol revealed.
- Click on the third finger from the right to raise it—again, note the symbol—and then go through the doorway.

SPIRAL STAIRCASE

- Approach the staircase and click on the handle.
- After you descend to the lower level, step forward and turn back to face the staircase.
- If you try to climb back up the staircase, you can't—you slide back down. Click on the crank handle in the middle of the room to transform the slide into steps.
- Climb the stairway to the main level.
- Turn left and continue climbing to the tower level.

TOWER

Four telescopes gaze out in different directions through the tower windows.

- Look through each telescope, beginning with the leftmost one. Note the structure in each view and the symbol etched on each lens:

The first telescope on the left is trained on what appears to be the Castle Irondune. The ▼ symbol is the one we've come to associate with Kaine and the earth element.

The second telescope focuses on the towering Asylum, and the view includes the ▽ symbol associated with Doctor Sartorius and the air element.

The third telescope is trained on the Conservatory and displays the ▲ symbol associated with Sophia Hamilton and the water element.

The fourth telescope is trained on the towering, pious spires of the Steppinthrax Monastery. The △ symbol is associated, of course, with Bishop Malveaux and the fire element.

℘ Go back down both flights of stairs.

MINE COMPLEX

℘ Go forward through the doorway. Another telescope!

℘ Use the telescope. It's trained on an odd, black, skull-shaped rock. And there's Kaine's earth symbol in the lens again. Hmmm. Exit the telescope view.

℘ Turn right to face the stairs, then climb them.

℘ Click on the control box (left of the mining car) for a close-up.

Do those building outlines look familiar? You just saw them through the tower telescopes. OK, remember that we're looking for the earth element. And remember who we're trying to liberate. Who's the earth guy again?

℘ Click on the outline of General Kaine's Castle Irondune—for those of you who suffer from silhouette memory lapse syndrome, it's the one at the upper right.

- ℭ The outline of the building changes to the earth symbol. It lights up. Exit the close-up.
- ℭ Click on the mining car to ride it.
- ℭ When the car reaches its destination, turn right and climb the stairs to the really big skulls.
- ℭ Click on the weird black skull—the one you saw through the telescope—to trigger a teleport back to the altar in the main hall.

MAIN HALL (SARCOPHAGI)

- ℭ Click on the "earthen" triangle at the top of the circle.
- ℭ Approach Kaine's glowing sarcophagus (second from right).

Kaine appears in the sun sculpture above his sarcophagus. He talks about the elements, then mentions that the Nemesis murdered his son, Lucien. He begs you to find the place where the boy's soul rests.

AIR ELEMENT PUZZLE

Doctor Sartorius is the air guy—♃. Check the Nemesis sketch of the Temple in your handy Bivotar journal. The air symbol is tucked up in the northeast corner of the map. Head that way now.

MAIN HALL (SARCOPHAGI)

- ℭ Go to the right side of the raised platform and enter the doorway in the back corner of the hall.
- ℭ Step forward to the edge of the starfield and turn right to face the five colored horns on the pedestal.
- ℭ Approach the pedestal.
- ℭ Click on each horn and listen to the elemental sound it

contains. Which one sounds like the element you're trying to find?

℘ That's right, the blue horn. Back away from the pedestal and go down to the starfield.

℘ Did you notice the air symbol in the blue star region? You need to light up only the blue stars. Note that clicking on some stars activates or deactivates other stars. But it won't take long to get only blue stars lit.

℘ Climb the spiral staircase that drops down.

℘ In the room at the top, go to the right side of the wind jar and turn to face the jar.

℘ Click on the wind jar for a close-up.

℘ Click on the black scarab (the bug just right of center) on the base of the wind jar.

℘ Now go back to the lever controls at the front of the wind jar and click on them for a close-up.

℘ Pure elemental air is clear. So the idea here is to mix the colored gases to create a clear wind jar.

℘ Drag the second lever to the middle notch.

℘ Drag the third and fourth levers all the way down to the bottom notch.

℘ Click on the tornado created in the wind jar. This triggers a teleportation back to the altar in the main hall.

MAIN HALL (SARCOPHAGI)

℘ Click on the air symbol at the left.

℘ Go towards Sartorius' now-glowing sarcophagus (first one on the left) and listen to his greeting.

Sartorius explains that he and the others are alchemists whose knowledge the Nemesis now seeks for "his own dark purposes."

He, too, begs for your help. Sartorius is a little creepier than the others, isn't he? But his record seems to speak for good. So OK, we'll help. As long as he gives us a little hit of that stuff he's breathing with such obvious pleasure. It's only fair.

Are you with me on this?

WATER ELEMENT PUZZLE

Sophia Hamilton needs her water element, man. She needs it bad. And you're just the person to get it for her.

MAIN HALL (SARCOPHAGI)

- ℭ After Sartorius' message, veer off to the left of the main raised platform.
- ℭ Go toward the stairway. (There's a steel grate in the middle of the stairs, if that's any help.)

UNTIL YOU SOLVE THE NEXT PART OF THE PUZZLE, EACH DOOR OPENS TO A STAIRWAY THAT SIMPLY LEADS YOU BACK TO WHERE YOU STARTED.

℃ Climb the stairs. At the top, you face two doors.

℃ Turn left and click on the "piper" sculpture. Listen carefully to the three-note chord that it plays.

℃ Turn around to face the fountain sculpture. You need to replicate the chord by clicking on the correct trio of fonts. (Wait, I forgot, this is a cheat book. From the left, click on fonts number 1, 4, and 5.) Hear that sound? You triggered something.

℃ Turn left to face the doors, and then go through the left door.

℃ Climb the stairs to the Water Room.

WATER ROOM

℃ Approach the hourglass in the center of the room.

℃ Click on the hourglass to turn it over.

℃ Yes, that's a chair. Sit in it.

℃ Spin left 360 degrees to face the door. You'll hear chimes and the sound of workers constructing something. Continue spinning left another 180 degrees to face the window. (The light above the window is yellow.)

℃ Take one step forward to the window.

℃ Take the saw.

℃ Sit back down on the chair.

℃ Spin left again. Chimes ring when you face the door, and you hear the roar of flames. Spin left further. The window has changed to a volcanic scene. (The light above the window is now red.)

℃ Continue spinning to the left two full rotations until you see an Ice Age scene in the window, with icicles hanging down.

℃ Take one step forward to the window.

- Use the saw on the longest icicle—the one hanging right over the bowl. A piece of ice falls into the bowl.
- Sit back down in the chair.
- Spin rightward until you return to the volcanic scene in the window. (Two full spins ought to do it.)
- Go forward to the window and watch the ice melt in the bowl.
- Quickly now, approach the bowl and then click on it. This triggers a teleportation back to the altar in the main hall.

WARNING! IF YOU WAIT TOO LONG AFTER THE ICE MELTS TO APPROACH THE BOWL, THE WATER EVAPORATES . . . AND YOU HAVE TO START ALL OVER AGAIN!

MAIN HALL (SARCOPHAGI)

- Click on the water symbol at the bottom of the screen.
- If you have not solved the other three element puzzles, go towards Sophia's now-glowing sarcophagus (first one on the left) and listen to her greeting.

23

If you are following this walk-through, however, you've found the last of the four elements. Thus, instead of a solo speech by Sophia, you view an appearance by all four alchemists. You also get a chilling message from the Nemesis. And, most important, you receive a gift from the alchemists—a model sun.

(｢ Go to the planetarium behind the raised altar platform.

PLANETARIUM

(｢ Go down the stairs to the lever controls.

(｢ Drag the left lever to its rightmost position. The mechanical arm moves toward you.

(｢ Place the model sun in the compartment.

(｢ Drag the left lever to its topmost position. The mechanical arm places the sun in the center of the solar system.

(｢ Drag the right lever clockwise just a bit, until you hear a "ding!" This triggers a fantastic teleport to the Steppinthrax Zorkastrian Monastery.

24

CHAPTER TWO

STEPPINTHRAX MONASTERY

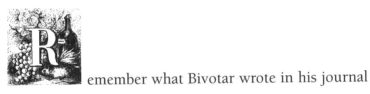emember what Bivotar wrote in his journal about "unbearable heat"? Seems an understatement, doesn't it? What a godforsaken place to put a home for holy guys. Your job here is to find the alchemical essence of Malveaux's metal, lead. Good luck. Don't get burned.

FIRST
THINGS FIRST.
WHEN YOU ARRIVE,
TURN COMPLETELY
AROUND. SEE THAT
MODEL OF THE PLANET
SATURN? **DON'T TOUCH
IT** . . . UNLESS YOU
WANT TO GO BACK
TO THE TEMPLE
PLANETARIUM.

LOWER COURTYARD

- Upon arrival, turn right and go through the archway.
- Read the plaque on the wall to your left, if you want. But the more important move here is to turn back to the archway and look down.
- Click on the glow and then pick up the coin that appears.
- Go forward through both archways and climb the stairs. Lovely view, isn't it?
- Continue up the stairs to the upper courtyard.

UPPER COURTYARD

⟨ Approach the monastery door. Try it; it's locked.

⟨ Turn right and go forward to the hole.

⟨ Go down the hole into the monastery.

MAIN HALL

⟨ Turn around and click on the sign next to the door. Read it and exit the close-up.

⟨ Prescience is a good thing, so click on the coin box for a close-up and put the coin (from the lower courtyard) into the coin slot at the top.

⟨ Take the slips of paper. Be sure to note the "6 Emotions" and their physical expressions, drawn as simple glyphs, as shown below.

Fear

Anger

Boredom

Happiness

Love

Suspicion

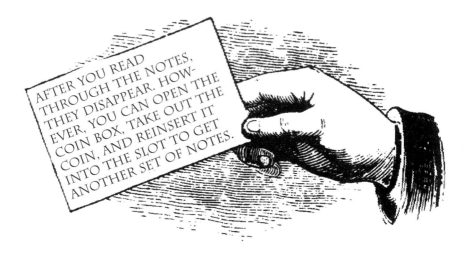

AFTER YOU READ THROUGH THE NOTES, THEY DISAPPEAR. HOWEVER, YOU CAN OPEN THE COIN BOX, TAKE OUT THE COIN, AND REINSERT IT INTO THE SLOT TO GET ANOTHER SET OF NOTES.

ℭ Go down the center aisle of the hall and climb the stairs.

ℭ Turn right to face the three masks on the wall. Click on them for a close-up.

Each face represents one of the "6 Emotions" noted in the messages you got from the coin box. Note that each mask has an empty slot just underneath it.

ℭ Exit the close-up of the masks.

ℭ Click on either urn to look inside. See the plaques? Do their glyphs look familiar?

There are two plaques in each urn, for a total of eight. You need to pick the six that correspond to the "6 Emotions" in the coin box glyphs, then match them up to the appropriate masks on the walls. Need help? Refer to the glyph illustrations on the previous page (or your own glyph sketches), and read on.

The masks on the left wall should be matched up with the following plaques, from left to right: Fear, Anger, Boredom.

 The masks on the right wall should be matched up with the following plaques, from left to right: Happiness, Love, Suspicion.

Once you place all six plaques correctly, the faces speak the lines of a poem. *Note the speaking order of the faces!* (The order is Anger, Suspicion, Love, Boredom, Fear, Happiness. Aren't cheat books so very convenient?) This order will be important later.

 Go forward and turn right.

 Climb the stairs and go through the door that lies just ahead.

SHRINE ROOM

 Cross the room to the odd shrine (although it may be a portable restroom, I can't tell). This triggers an encounter with a mad monk.

 Turn right and enter the next room.

 Click on the empty basin to trigger a vision of the alchemists performing an exotic baptism.

 Head over to the back right corner and look down at the grate.

 Click twice on the grate to reveal the paper.

 Click on the paper to examine it.

Notice that the letters of the words on the left side of the page correspond in number to the glyphs at right. This is a simple code. Search the code words to find each letter of the word at the top of

the page—"OPEN"—and then find the corresponding glyph. You end up with the following sequence of glyphs:

℃ Return to the hallway.

℃ Go straight ahead into the bell tower.

BELL TOWER

℃ Climb the winding staircase.

℃ Turn slightly right and head just left of the mechanism.

℃ At the sheet of bell sequences, turn right and follow the walkway to the door.

℃ Go through the door into the monk residence hall.

MONK RESIDENCE HALL

℃ Malveaux's room on the middle of the left side is boarded up. You'll have to find another way to get in.

℃ Despite all the doors, you can enter only one residence—Alexandria's, which is the third room from the end of the hall on the right side.

ALEXANDRIA'S ROOM

℃ Cross the room to the bed and click on the violin.

℃ Read the diary on the ledge just left of the bed.

- Approach the music stand and click on the sheet music to see a vision of Malveaux and Alexandria.

- Exit into the hall, turn right, and go through the door at the end of the hall.

MALVEAUX'S OFFICE

- Go forward to the desk, turn left, and explore the alcove that lies straight ahead.

- Open the medical book and read the four intriguing notes from Sartorius. The first is dated 922. Apparently, Malveaux was suffering from an incurable cancer, and he joined with Sartorius in seeking the "quintessence."

- Explore further down the alcove.

- Take the odd magnifying glass.

- Go across the back of the room and turn into the desk area.

- Read the note from Malveaux regarding the "Implementor's Eye"—gee, could that be the odd glass you just picked up?

- Now click on the exotic smoking device—that's what I see in it, anyway—to trigger a vision of Malveaux, Sartorius, and Sophia Hamilton speaking of the Nemesis.

- Exit the desk area, turn right, and examine the alcove on the right side of the office. Read the two letters from Sophia regarding Alexandria's stay at the Conservatory.

- Turn right and go further down the alcove.

- Open the book, *On Immortality*, and read the note from Sartorius.

- Exit the office and return to the bell tower.

STEPPINTHRAX MONASTERY

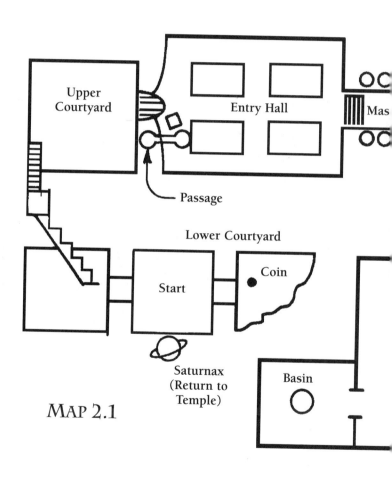

Upper Courtyard

Entry Hall

Mas

Passage

Lower Courtyard

Start

Coin

Saturnax
(Return to
Temple)

Basin

MAP 2.1

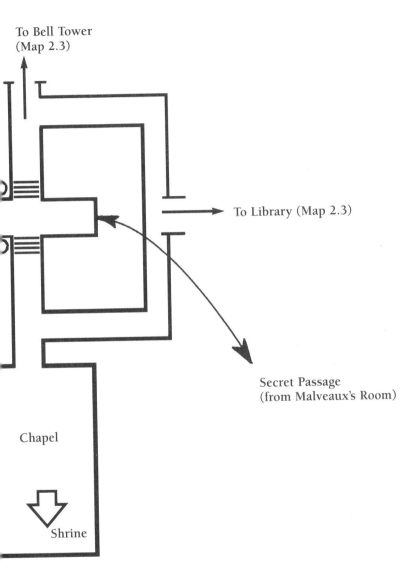

To Bell Tower
(Map 2.3)

To Library (Map 2.3)

Secret Passage
(from Malveaux's Room)

Chapel

Shrine

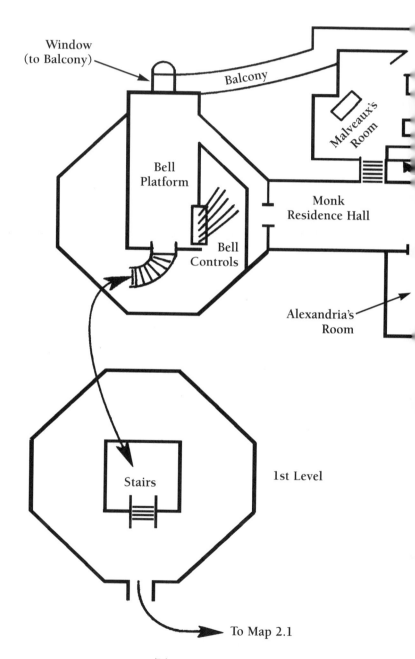

Window
(to Balcony)

Balcony

Malveaux's
Room

Bell
Platform

Bell
Controls

Monk
Residence Hall

Alexandria's
Room

Stairs

1st Level

To Map 2.1

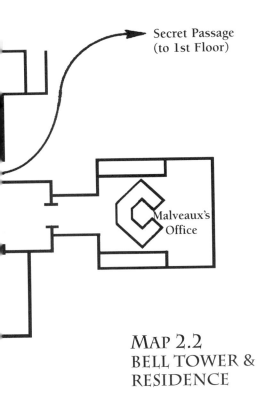

Secret Passage
(to 1st Floor)

Malveaux's
Office

MAP 2.2
BELL TOWER &
RESIDENCE

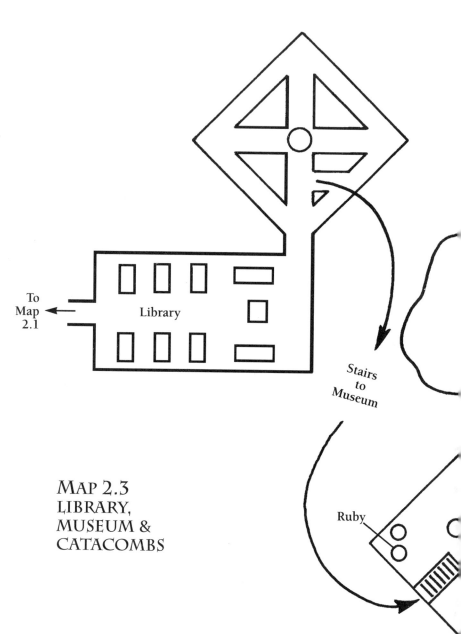

To
Map
2.1

Library

Stairs
to
Museum

MAP 2.3
LIBRARY,
MUSEUM &
CATACOMBS

Ruby

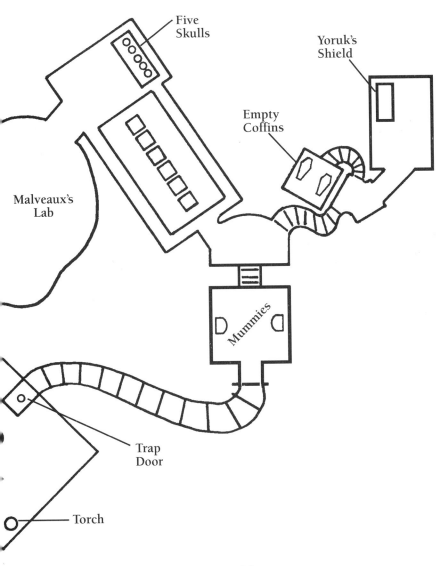

Five
Skulls

Yoruk's
Shield

Empty
Coffins

Malveaux's
Lab

Mummies

Trap
Door

Torch

BELL TOWER

℘ Follow the walkway back to the sheet of paper tacked on the wall.

Uh-oh, those darn glyphs again. Note the pattern for "The Seventh Bell"—five missing glyphs, then the glyph for Happiness. Where can you find a six-glyph code, ending in Happiness? Ah, remember the poem spoken by the masks? Remember the order in which they spoke? You don't? Hey, it's OK, neither do I. Fortunately, we jotted them down earlier.

℘ Go to the bell control mechanism.

℘ Click on the controls in the following order—Anger, Suspicion, Love, Boredom, Fear, Happiness.

℘ When the bellrope drops, click on it for close-up.

℘ Click on the rope to ring the "Seventh Bell." Note that when you ring the bell, you hang onto the rope, which jerks you up and down. Note also that you catch a very quick glimpse of a window each time you jerk upward.

℘ Keep ringing the bell. Each time you see the window, try to click on it. It may take several tries, but eventually you'll hop through the window to the balcony outside.

℘ Follow the balcony around the corner to the open door, and then enter Malveaux's room.

MALVEAUX'S ROOM

℘ Take two steps forward towards the door, then turn left and take a step toward the bed.

❧ Click on the flame tapestry above the bed. Note the order of the flame colors, from left to right—blue, yellow, red, orange, white. As usual, this will be very important later. Exit the close-up.

❧ Click on the scrapbook sitting on the nightstand just to the right of the bed. Some very interesting correspondences accompany the photos of young Alexandria. What's going on here? You also learn of the girl's budding romance with Lucien Kaine.

❧ Now click on the book that lies on the bed.

❧ Activate the magic glass (the "Implementor's Eye") from your inventory and use it on the red page of the book.

❧ Click on the glass for a close-up look at an arrangement of skulls. Beginning at the upper left, note, in order, which directions the skulls face—south, west, southeast, southwest, east. Again, this will be important later.

❧ Exit the close-up of the book and head towards the small table across the room.

❧ Click on the table for a close-up of the amulet.

❧ Click on the amulet to see a vision of Bishop Malveaux at prayer. He indicates that he's paid quite a price for his search for immortality. What might that price be? Note where the amulet rests when the vision dissipates.

❧ Go to the bookshelf to the right of the door.

❧ Read the journal on the middle shelf.

❧ Now go to the bookshelf on the other side of the door.

❧ Click on the faded book to open a secret passage down to the entry hall.

LOOK AROUND AND
NOTE WHERE YOU
ARRIVE. THIS IS NOW
A TWO-WAY PASSAGE.
TO RETURN TO
MALVEAUX'S ROOM,
SIMPLY GO THROUGH
THE WALL AT THE
END OF THE ALCOVE.

❦ Take the first right and follow the corridor around until you reach the library on the left-hand side of the corridor.

LIBRARY

❦ Go straight down the aisle to the lectern and open Brother Malveaux's book, *St. Yoruk.* Watch the vision—Malveaux is about to conduct a wedding ceremony for his adopted daughter Alexandria and Kaine's son, Lucien.

❦ Turn left and read all the texts that surround the lectern, beginning with book on the left. Go around clockwise to learn the story of Yoruk. Note carefully how Yoruk survives his trial by fire using a bronze shield studded with rubies.

❦ Turn left and go through the door at the back of the room.

MUSEUM (UPPER LEVEL)

- You emerge onto a walkway above a museum. Go forward a step and turn right to the gate. Locked, doggon-it!

- Continue to the pedestal in the center of the room and click on it for a close-up.

- Glyphs! Ye gads, not again. Do these look familiar? Yes, of course they do. Get out your glyph code for the word "OPEN" and click on each one in order— ∞ ⚥ ♋ ⚚ . You hear something unlock.

- Turn around and go back to the gate. Unlocked! Open the gate and go downstairs.

MUSEUM (LOWER LEVEL)

- There's a lot of stuff to see, but I'll be concise here. Turn left, then head past the sign to the left corner of the room.

- Take the Ruby From Yoruk's Shield.

- Turn left and head toward the corner with the shield replica.

- Take the Torch of the Endless Fire—nice joke, don't you think?

- Now go to that odd covered basin (looks like a closed barbecue grill) in the center of the room.

- Click on the basin to open it.

- Click on any knob to deactivate the alarm system. (This also unlocks the trapdoor.)

- Turn left and look down at the trapdoor.

- Click on the trapdoor to open it and go downstairs to the catacombs.

CATACOMBS

- ℭ Talk to the mummies on either side of the passage. They speak of Yoruk's shield, flames all around, "the perfect stone," and so on. Keep their comments in mind as you proceed down the passage.
- ℭ Don't go down that red glowing passage to the left yet! The Nemesis will burn you alive if you're not prepared. Instead, take the passage to the right.
- ℭ Go through the open iron gate.

COFFIN ROOM

- ℭ Don't go forward into the darkness yet! (You'll get devoured in a most gruesome fashion.) Instead, approach the burning torch on the opposite wall.
- ℭ Click the Torch of the Endless Fire (from the museum— you got it, didn't you?) on the burning torch. This lights your torch.
- ℭ Back away from the wall torch and turn left. See that coffin?
- ℭ Go to the coffin. At this point, you can either hang onto your torch or put it in the torch holder on the wall across from the coffin. (You can see better if you keep the torch.)
- ℭ Open the coffin and get in.
- ℭ Click on the lid to close it. Hey, is that a shield up there?
- ℭ Put the ruby (from the museum) in the missing center slot of the shield.
- ℭ Take the shield.
- ℭ Click on the lid to open the coffin, and then get out.
- ℭ Exit the coffin room, climb the stairs, and go into the glowing red room.

DEMON FIRE ROOM

- ❦ Activate Yoruk's Shield from your inventory. And steel yourself... it's hell in here.
- ❦ Take a step forward.
- ❦ After the demon speaks, use Yoruk's Shield on the fire.
- ❦ Go forward, turn right, and approach the five skulls.
- ❦ Remember your skull sequence from the book on Malveaux's bed? In order from left to right, the skulls need to face south, west, southeast, southwest, and east. For the weak of mind, here's how:

> Leave the first skull alone.
>
> Turn the second skull two clicks to the left.
>
> Turn the third skull one click to the right.
>
> Turn the fourth skull one click to the left.
>
> Turn the fifth skull two clicks to the right.

- ❦ Turn around and enter Malveaux's now-open laboratory.

MALVEAUX'S LAB

- ❦ Go to the alcove on the left wall.
- ❦ Take the key and the piece of metal (looks like a drill bit).
- ❦ Optional: Read the book.
- ❦ Continue along the left wall to the big egg-shaped contraption.
- ❦ Click on the small door in the wall (right of the egg thing) for a close-up, and then click on the handle to open the door.
- ❦ Put the key in the keyhole.

⟨ Click on the key to turn it.

⟨ Back away from the door and click on the knob handle of the podium at the right. This opens the egg and reveals a cup.

⟨ Put the metal drill bit into the cup.

⟨ Click the handle to close the egg.

⟨ After the egg twists and stops, click the handle again to open the egg.

⟨ Take the lead ball from the cup.

⟨ Cross to the opposite side of the room and click on the bubbling vat for a close-up. (Golfers out there may recognize this as a medieval ball washer.)

⟨ Put the lead ball in the container and exit the close-up.

⟨ Click on the pulley weight at right to lower the container into the vat.

⟨ Click on the vat again and take the now-polished lead ball.

⟨ Go back across the room and approach the wheel valve.

⟨ Click on the wheel to turn the valve and start the lava flow.

⟨ Turn around and approach the lion's head.

To refine the lead to its essence, you need to set, precisely, the temperature of the flames on the right side of the coil tube. Here's where you put that flame tapestry above Malveaux's bed to use.

⟨ From top to bottom, click on the control boxes to set the flames to the following colors (from top to bottom)—blue, yellow, red, orange, white.

⟨ Put the polished ball in the lion's mouth.

⟨ Look down into the receptacle and *quickly* use the bellows to cool the metal into the shape of the elemental symbol. (If you wait too long, the metal cools back into its original corkscrew shape, and you have to start all over again.)

℘ Take the elemental lead. This triggers a somewhat fiery teleport back to the altar in the main hall of the Temple.

TEMPLE ALTAR

℘ Click on the lead elemental symbol. This fills the center receptacle with a blood-red liquid.

℘ Click on the center receptacle and watch the disturbing vision.

℘ Click on Malveaux's glowing sarcophagus to hear his message. He reiterates that you must bring them the four metals.

℘ Go to the planetarium.

TEMPLE PLANETARIUM

Drag the handle on the right podium clockwise until you hear the second ding. This triggers a journey to the Frigid River Branch Conservatory of Madame Sophia Hamilton.

CHAPTER THREE

FRIGID RIVER BRANCH CONSERVATORY

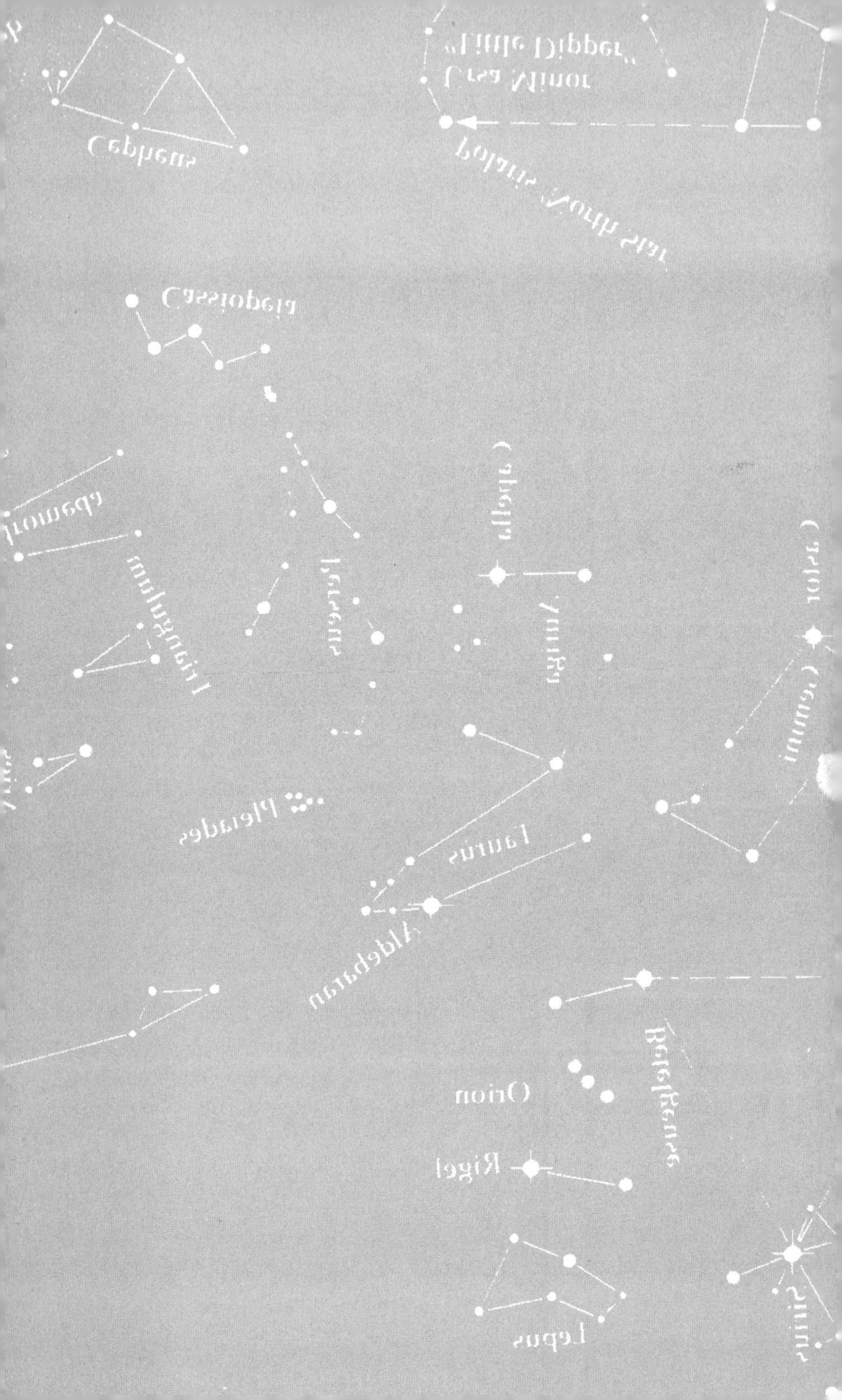

Cepheus

Cassiopeia

Andromeda

Triangulum

Pleiades

Capella

Auriga

Perseus

Cetus (Whale)

Taurus

Aldebaran

Orion

Betelgeuse

Rigel

Lepus

Sirius

Little Dipper

Polaris, the North Star

Bivotar's journal speaks of this liquid place, saying "it was almost as if I could hear lingering melodies from years ago." Almost? Open your ears, man. Music is *everywhere* in this haunted place. You arrive on an outer balcony of the conservatory. Behind you is the spinning orb of Venusnv, which you can use to teleport back to the Temple planetarium if you so desire. Remember, your job here is to find Sophia's metal, copper, and distill its pure essence.

OUTER BALCONY

⟨ Enter the building.

⟨ If you want, you can go straight up the stairs. You won't find much, though. They lead up to an uneventful hallway, which leads to more stairs, which bring you right back down.

⟨ Better idea: Turn right and head for the orchestra chart just to the left of the doorway on the far wall.

⟨ Sketch the chart.

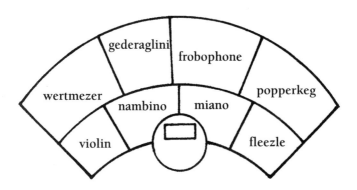

⟨ Turn around and step up onto the small practice stage.

PRACTICE STAGE

⟨ Look down at the floor to see the musical instruments. There are four instruments on the left and four more on the right.

⟨ Note how the chairs are also set up in groups of four on the left and four more on the right.

❦ Note also that you can pick up instruments and put them in the chairs.

Bivotar's journal refers to these musical instruments, and you can use his sketches and observations to identify each by name. The instruments on the left side are the violin, the nambino (drum), the fleezle (reed instrument), and the popperkeg (odd, popping percussion instrument). The instruments on the right side are the gederaglini (double horn), the wertmezer (accordion), the frobophone (horn), and the miano (lyre).

❦ Pick up each of the instruments. Memorize each one's sound (or take really good notes regarding these characteristics).

❦ Now arrange the instruments on the chairs, placing them according to the arrangement on the orchestra chart:

On the left side:

Front Row—violin left, nambino right

Back Row—wertmezer left, gederaglini right

On the right side:

Front Row—miano left, fleezle right

Back Row—frobophone left, popperkeg right

After you place the instruments correctly, you hear Sophia speaking to Alexandria of the notes which constitute the Harmony of the Spheres—C, D, E, B, and G. Let's jot down that note progression, shall we? Needless to say, this bit of information will be crucial later.

❦ Step off the stage, turn left, and examine the record player on the left. No records!

❦ Continue down the hall and go through the door.

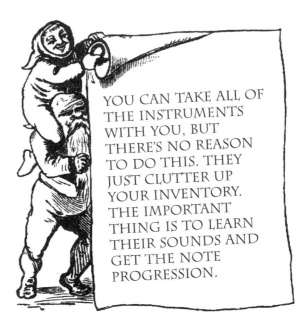

YOU CAN TAKE ALL OF THE INSTRUMENTS WITH YOU, BUT THERE'S NO REASON TO DO THIS. THEY JUST CLUTTER UP YOUR INVENTORY. THE IMPORTANT THING IS TO LEARN THEIR SOUNDS AND GET THE NOTE PROGRESSION.

MAIN HALL

- ℂ Cross to the opposite side of the main hall.
- ℂ Turn right and click on the ticket booth for a close-up. The ticket tray is empty.
- ℂ Turn around and go into the office.

SOPHIA'S OFFICE

- ℂ Go to the table on the right side of the room—the one with the lighted blue lamp on it.
- ℂ Open the small wooden box on the table and take the tuning fork.
- ℂ Look in the album rack to the right of the desk.

- Flip through the records until you get to "Introduction to the Orchestra." Take it.
- Take the next album, too—"Alexandria Wolfe, Debut Album."
- Go around to the front of the piano.
- Click on the small box at the left side of the piano.
- In the close-up, put the tuning fork (from the desk) into the hole on the top of the box.
- Exit the close-up and then click on the keyboard for an overhead shot.
- Click on the tuning fork and listen carefully to the tone.
- Now play the note on the piano (the A above middle C). The key klunks and you hear something fall.
- Go behind the piano and look in at the strings.
- Take the key.
- Turn slightly right and examine the green book, "On Music and Perfection," sitting on the desk. You find information about various instruments.
- Go around the big desk. (You have to go around on the right-hand side.)
- Click on the desk for a full view, and then open the bottom right-hand drawer.
- Read the series of notes from Malveaux to Sophia.

What is this "Harmony of the Spheres" that keeps popping up in all the correspondence? And why so much concern about Alexandria's affair with Lucien Kaine? Also note the letters from Sartorius, which speak of generating crystals, using small crystals as "seeds for growth," and increasing crystal purity by dissolving calcium bromide.

❦ OK, now open the bottom left-hand drawer and read the notes from Kaine.

Kaine obviously has a thing for Sophia. In these letters, we learn that his war is not going well—and that he is disturbed by his son Lucien's suspicious behavior. There's also a curious note from someone named Brog which mentions a lamp key slot. Hmmm.

❦ Exit the drawer close-up and click on the desktop.

❦ Activate that key you found in the piano, then click it on the small slot in the stem of the lamp.

❦ Click on the cord to turn on the lamp. Aha! A note and a map!

The note has instructions. Read them carefully, and write them down: "Prepare the boiling solution, seed with crystal, purify the crystal, ring the notes together." (Jot down the map of rooms, too, if you're one of those self-starter types.)

❦ Exit the office.

MAIN HALL

❦ Step forward into the center of the main hall.

❦ For fun, let's turn right and approach the door to the auditorium.

❦ Click on the door a couple of times to get turned away. After the second rejection, the door is locked.

❦ The other doors on the lower level of the hall are locked, too, including the one to the Boiler Room.

❦ Before you go, check out the torn poster to the right of the Boiler Room door. Click on it. It advertises Alexandria Wolfe performing "Harmony of the Spheres!"

❦ Go up the stairs just to the left of the Boiler Room door.

MAIN HALL (UPPER WALKWAY)

(At the top of the stairs, turn right and follow the walkway .

(Enter the first door on the right.

DORMITORY

(Turn right, go to the far end of the room, and then turn left to face the bed.

(Click on the large scrapbook on the bed.

(Page through the concert posters until you reach the last one— Alexandria's "Harmony of the Spheres" poster again!

(Take the poster and exit the close-up.

(Look down at the floor.

(Click on the darkened floorboard to pull it up.

(Read the letters from Lucien.

Lucien's letters speak of his father's war against Ellron and the Enchanter's Guild. It mentions something called Thaddium and a new invention that "involves pure lead."

(Look up and approach the desk by the window.

(Read the excerpts from both books.

The Musings on the Power of Melody speaks of five essential musical notes. The other book, *Path to Musical Perfection*, speaks once again of the mysterious Harmony of the Spheres . . . and says if it is played "with a Hand both Pure and Worthe," something amazing will happen. Are you beginning to see why everyone wants Alexandria to ditch the Kaine kid?

(Turn right to face the vanity.

(Click on the small hand mirror to view a scene between Sophia and Alexandria.

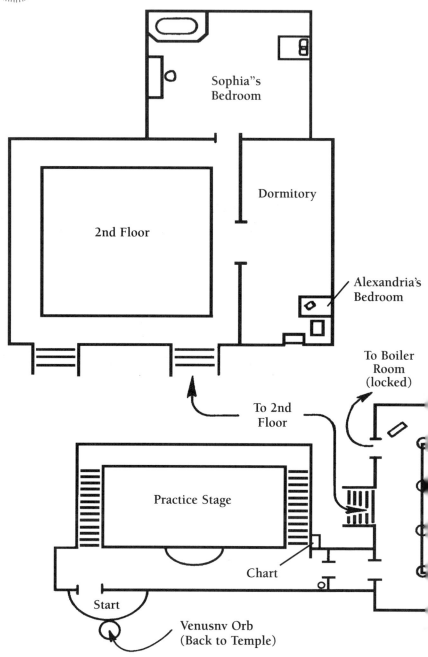

FRIGID RIVER BRANCH CONSERVATORY

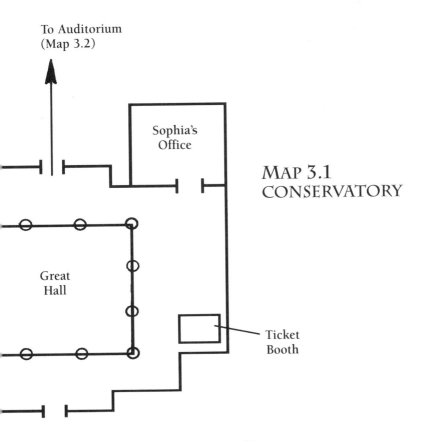

To Auditorium
(Map 3.2)

Sophia's
Office

MAP 3.1
CONSERVATORY

Great
Hall

Ticket
Booth

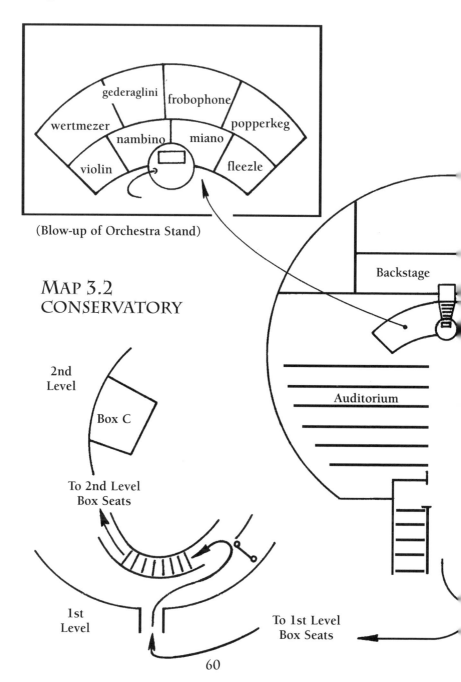

(Blow-up of Orchestra Stand)

MAP 3.2
CONSERVATORY

2nd
Level

Box C

To 2nd Level
Box Seats

Backstage

Auditorium

1st
Level

To 1st Level
Box Seats

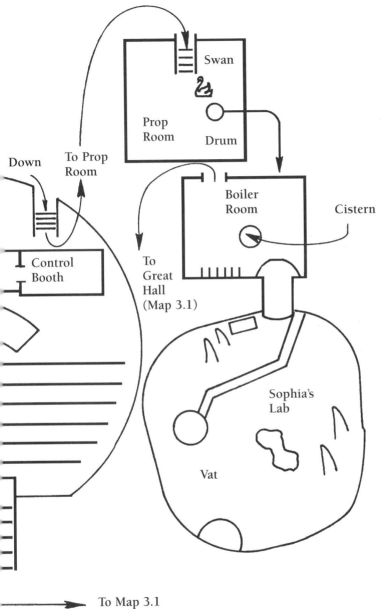

Swan

Prop
Room

Drum

Down

To Prop
Room

Control
Booth

Boiler
Room

Cistern

To
Great
Hall
(Map 3.1)

Sophia's
Lab

Vat

To Map 3.1
(Great Hall)

❧ Click on the music box, and then on its key to open the box.

❧ Look inside and click on the red felt to watch the scene with Lucien, Alexandria, and Sophia. Bummer about the locket. Where'd it go?

❧ Exit the dormitory. Turn right and go straight into Sophia's room.

SOPHIA'S ROOM

❧ Go to the vanity and read the letters. Kind of disturbing about Kaine, wouldn't you say? He seems to want the Philosopher Stone for power's sake, and his wife doesn't have much good to say about him.

❧ Pull back the partition next to the vanity to reveal the tub.

❧ Look in the tub and watch a PG-13 scene with Kaine and Sophia. Clearly, it's immortality they seek—and not exactly for the most noble of reasons.

❧ Go to the right of the tub area.

❧ Pick up and read the book entitled *Alchemy*.

Again, here's evidence of some "singular array of notes" which, when played by a pure hand, will cause a magical event to happen—"a chain of perfect effect and proportion." Terra, Aqua, Aer, Ignis—C, D, E, B. Said to be the Harmony of the Spheres.

❧ Exit the room, and then go back downstairs to the record player in the practice hall.

PRACTICE HALL

❧ Play Alexandria's debut album, and listen very carefully to the order of instruments in the closing Zorkian Fanfare.

IF YOU NEED HELP IDENTIFYING THE INSTRUMENTS, PICK UP THE INSTRUMENTS ON THE PRACTICE STAGE OR LISTEN TO THE "INTRODUCTION TO THE ORCHESTRA" ALBUM.

The fanfare order:

popperkeg

nambino

popperkeg

wertmezer

violin

℮ Go back to the torn poster of Alexandria in the great hall.

GREAT HALL

℮ Use the poster from Alexandria's scrapbook to replace the torn poster. Hear the voices? Concert time!

℮ Go to the ticket window and click on the concert ticket that now sits in the ticket slot.

❦ In the close-up, note that your seat is Box C. Now take the ticket to put it in inventory.

❦ Go to the Auditorium door and click your concert ticket on the door. After the woman takes your ticket and disappears, follow her in.

AUDITORIUM

❦ Go up the stairs to the first level of box seats.

❦ Follow the corridor to the right.

❦ At the roped-off area, turn around and climb the next set of stairs to the second level of box seats.

❦ From the top of the stairs, follow the corridor around to Box C, then enter.

BOX SEAT C

❦ Sit down and pick up the concert glasses.

❦ After Alexandria gives her performance, put down the glasses and exit the box.

❦ Go back down to the main floor of the auditorium.

AUDITORIUM

❦ Restless patrons are calling for the standard Zorkian Conclusory Fanfare! (The lights won't go on until the fanfare is played.)

❦ Go straight down the aisle, up to the conductor's perch.

CONDUCTOR'S STAND

- ℚ Take the baton from the stand.

- ℚ Remember your orchestra chart? You have to click in the dark on this one, and it may take some experimenting before you get it right. But don't worry . . . nobody's going anywhere until you do. (It's the Zork way.)

This is a tricky puzzle. You have to use the baton to elicit the proper sequence of instruments to play the fanfare. From playing Alexandria's debut album, you know that the correct order is *popperkeg, nambino, popperkeg, wertmezer, violin.* From the orchestra chart you know (roughly) where each instrument is located in front of you.

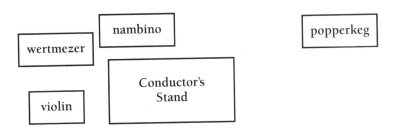

- ℚ Click the baton on each instrument location in the correct order of the fanfare.

- ℚ After the lights come on, go through the curtains to get backstage.

BACKSTAGE

- ℚ Go to the left side of the stage.

- ℚ On the second box along the back wall, find and read an intriguing note to Lucien from Alexandria.

℃ Turn around and go along the backdrop until you find the hole in the lower corner. Unfortunately, other lowered backdrops block the hole. How can we raise these things?

℃ Go back to the curtains, turn left, and enter the stage control booth.

STAGE CONTROL BOOTH

℃ Look at the buttons on the control panel. What the heck do they operate?

℃ Click on the clipboard at the far right.

Your goal here is to get behind the backdrops. The pictures on the clipboard depict the seven backdrops that are raised by pressing the corresponding blue buttons on the control panel. You need to raise all of the backdrops that have no hole in the lower right-hand corner.

℃ Flip through the pictures. Backdrops 1 (undersea scene), 5 (checkerboard garden), and 7 (riverside hut) all have holes in the lower right corner, so you can leave those down. The other backdrops need to be raised.

℃ Exit the clipboard close-up and click on the red button to activate the control panel.

℃ Note that button 1 has blown out. From left to right, click on buttons 2, 3, 4, and 6 to raise the corresponding backdrops.

℃ Go back to the hole in the backdrop, climb through, and head down the stairs to the right.

PROP ROOM

Remember the sketch of this room on the desk in Sophia's office? The boiler room is directly below somewhere, but how do we get to it? Hang with me, man.

- Approach that old-fashioned Zorktone radio across the room and click on the VOL switch to turn it on. You hear Sophia repeat a phrase over and over: "Your locket?"
- Go back to the foot of the stairs, turn around, and step toward the swan. You hop onto its back.
- Turn right and click on the crank handle.
- Turn left and look down at the really big drum.
- Jump onto the drum. Surprise!

BOILER ROOM

- Look down, and then step forward toward the cistern.
- Try to take the locket. Ooops!
- Look in the cistern. That's deep stuff. What now?
- Right. Dive in the cistern.
- Sea hunt! When you reach bottom, look down and grab the locket.
- You can look up and swim to the surface—but then you'd be a third-rate adventurer and a wuss. You have a reputation to uphold. Go straight ahead through that doorway under the clock.

SOPHIA'S LAB

℘ Wow! Click on crystals—each vibrates with a different note.

℘ Click on the green fishlike crystal and take the tablet it regurgitates.

℘ Go to the hole in the wall on the far side of the cavern and take a green crystal. Could this be one of the "seed crystals" mentioned in the notes you read earlier? Could it? Could it?

℘ Examine the chart on the wall. It shows you which crystals emit which notes.

Recall that Sophia spoke of the Harmony of the Spheres as a progression of notes—C, D, E, B, G. Son of a gun. Those are the very notes we see here in this chart. What a small world, but it seems we're missing a G crystal.

℘ Approach the vat. It's turned off, apparently, and it's got some kind of congealed formula in it. Follow the pipe that runs out of the vat to a door.

℘ Click on the door. Hey, the boiler room!

BOILER ROOM

OK, let's get to work. Consult the instructions from the desk in Sophia's office: "Prepare the boiling solution, seed with crystal, purify the crystal, ring the notes together." To prepare the boiling solution, we probably need to turn on the boiler.

℘ Go to the row of six valves on the wall.

℘ The only one that works is the second from the left, but it only stays open for a few seconds. So put Alexandria's locket on it to hold it open.

❦ Go back through the door into the lab.

SOPHIA'S LAB

❦ Put the green "seed crystal" into the now-bubbling vat. A big crystal emerges. Could this be the missing G crystal?

❦ Purify the new crystal by tossing the tablet (from the green fish crystal) into the vat.

❦ Music time! To make perfect harmony, consult the chart and then go around the lab and click the C, D, E, and B crystals.

❦ Return to the vat and click on the new crystal, a perfect G.

❦ After the new crystal breaks, look in the vat.

❦ Click on the pure metal symbol. This teleports you back to the Temple Altar.

TEMPLE ALTAR

❦ Click on the new elemental symbol. This fills the center receptacle with a blood-red liquid.

❦ Click on the center receptacle and watch the disturbing vision of Sophia's murder.

❦ Click on Sophia Hamilton's glowing sarcophagus to hear her message. She claims her actions were in good faith, but accepts guilt for what has occurred. She begs you to bring the remaining alchemical metals.

❦ Go to the planetarium.

TEMPLE PLANETARIUM

Drag the handle on the right podium counter-clockwise until you hear the second ding. This triggers a journey to the Castle Irondune, home of General Kaine.

CHAPTER FOUR

THE CASTLE IRONDUNE

In his journal, Bivotar writes at length about the state of siege that Irondune endures. He also mentions that General Thaddeus Kaine maneuvers his troops through an elaborate system of remote radio control codes. Keep this in mind as you search the castle. You arrive in a lookout post at the top of the castle. Behind you is the spinning orb of Murz (Mars). As with the other locations, you can use the orb to teleport back to the Temple planetarium.

CASTLE LOOKOUT POST

- ℭ Click on the black handle to lower the elevator.
- ℭ When the elevator stops, step out onto the balcony overlooking a big entry hall.

CASTLE ENTRY HALL

- ℭ Turn right and go down the stairs.
- ℭ Go through the first doorway on the right.
- ℭ Climb the stairs to first landing.

Note the locked door guarded by a suit of armor. Note also that you can raise and lower the helmet's visor.

- ℭ Enter the room just off the landing.

KAINE'S ROOM

- ℭ Just inside the door, turn right.
- ℭ Click on leftmost bookcase, second shelf from the top, and peruse the book titles. Not much of interest, but what the heck, we love to snoop.
- ℭ Step into the center of the room and turn left.
- ℭ Read the note on the front of the desk: "Order more nitro."
- ℭ Go behind the desk, turn around, and approach the desk.
- ℭ Click on the letter spike and read the friendly note from Lord Ellron. Can't you just see this guy strutting around, calling everyone a "girlyman"?
- ℭ Open the right-hand drawer and read the letters. What is this Thaddium stuff, anyway?
- ℭ Open the left-hand drawer and take the vial of nitro.

❦ Read the odd poem. It's a clue, big time, for later. So let's jot it down here:

> Five brave fellows stand
> guard over my dungeon;
> three are blind,
> two can see,
> but as a whole
> they form the key.

❦ Exit the drawer close-up and head directly across the room to the closed door.

❦ The door's locked, but swivel to the right and examine the objects on the side-stand—a book on encryption (note the circled phrase about encryption as "a game"), and a letter from Sartorius making reference to "injection molding."

❦ Turn around and examine the photo album (red book at left) on the opposite side-stand.

Pay attention to the note on the temperature of casting metal, and be sure to click on the news clippings to get a close-up for reading. At last we get a description of Thaddium—"lethal zirradiated ore."

❦ Read the excerpt in the book (tilted, at right) entitled The New Blood Alchemists.

❦ Go to the trunk at the foot of the bed and try to open it. Locked!

❦ Use the vial of nitro (from the desk) on the lock of the trunk.

❦ Open the trunk and examine its contents—fretful (and informative) letters from Sophia, an odd note about "weapons of assassination," and some extremely important battle plans for breaking the siege of Irondune.

❦ Go to the right side of the bed and click on the nightstand.

❦ Read Kaine's journal to learn of Lucien's odd behavior.

❦ Go around to the nightstand on the other side of the bed and check out the framed photos.

❦ Exit the room, turn left, climb the stairs to the next landing, and enter the room on the left.

GAMING ROOM

❦ Step to the center of the room, then veer left to the sign on the wall. It's an important clue! Write it down! No, wait . . . I'll do it for you:

First Button:
Candles and Broomsticks

Second Button:
Shaving a Cat

Third Button:
Fishing in the Desert

Fourth Button:
Triple Splitter

Fifth Button:
SHOOT!

❦ Click on the pool table for a close-up. Note the five buttons on the left.

Remember the circled passage in the encryption book (in Kaine's room) referring to encryption as a game? Here's a swell example. Buttons 1 through 4 each set up a particular pool shot noted on the sign above the table.

    🎵 To activate a particular pool shot: Click the button (1 to 4) that corresponds to that shot according to the sign. Then click on button 5 to shoot.

    🎵 Look at the balls in the tray after each shot and note the numerical order:

Shot 1: Candles and Broomsticks	1, 7, 4, 3, 5, 9
Shot 2: Shaving a Cat	4, 7, 1, 3, 9, 5
Shot 3: Fishing in the Desert	7, 4, 1, 9, 5, 3
Shot 4: Triple Splitter	4, 3, 5, 9, 7, 1

Could these be some sort of code? Duh.

    🎵 Ignore the foosball table, or not. (Nothing important happens.)

    🎵 Exit the room, head left down the stairs to the next landing.

    🎵 Note the locked door and the suit of armor, and enter the room on the left.

LUCIEN'S ROOM

    🎵 Step to the center of the room, turn right, and go examine the paintings—one on the wall (note the violin), one in the fireplace.

    🎵 Turn left and walk around the canvas on the easel.

    🎵 The canvas looks unused. But pick up the paintbrush and use it (click, hold, drag) to erase the coating over the canvas.

Aha! Another code! Write it down:

1. Build Bridge
2. Ambush
3. Dig Trenches
4. Latrine Cleaning
5. Coup d' Etat
6. Infiltrate & Destroy
7. Serve Mess
8. Burn & Pillage
9. Split the Troops
10. Distraction
11. Drop Thaddium
12. Verify Message

Remember the battle plans you found when you blew open Kaine's trunk? If you examine them carefully, you come up with a sequence of actions that match up to ones listed in the above code. Thus, you can translate the siege-breaking plan into a code sequence that goes 10, 1, 9, 6.

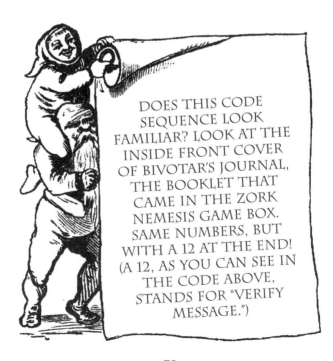

DOES THIS CODE SEQUENCE LOOK FAMILIAR? LOOK AT THE INSIDE FRONT COVER OF BIVOTAR'S JOURNAL, THE BOOKLET THAT CAME IN THE ZORK NEMESIS GAME BOX. SAME NUMBERS, BUT WITH A 12 AT THE END! (A 12, AS YOU CAN SEE IN THE CODE ABOVE, STANDS FOR "VERIFY MESSAGE.")

⟨ Turn and cross the room to the left side of the bed.

⟨ Read the draft notice tucked in the lower-left corner of the mirror.

⟨ Turn left to face the armoire.

⟨ Look down and take the gunpowder.

⟨ Read the note from Kaine to Lucien.

⟨ Now go examine the desk at the far end of the room.

⟨ Read the notes from Alexandria to Lucien, and about the deadly Thaddium explosion. Note the concert ticket.

⟨ Exit the room, turn right, and go down the stairs back to the castle entry hall.

CASTLE ENTRY HALL

⟨ Approach the large front door and click on it a few times to see the old guard. He won't let you out. Worse, he calls you a dumb hungus.

⟨ Turn around and go through the doorway under the center of the stairway.

GREAT HALL

⟨ Just inside the doorway, turn right and pick up the broken sword hilt sitting on the arm of the chair.

⟨ Turn around and approach the rear of the gold dog "statue."

⟨ In the close-up of the tail end, click on the dog's bottom (not the tail) to open it, and then click again to look inside. It's a cannon aimed at the door!

⟨ Drop the gunpowder (from Lucien's room) inside.

⟨ Exit and close the dog's bottom.

Map 4.1

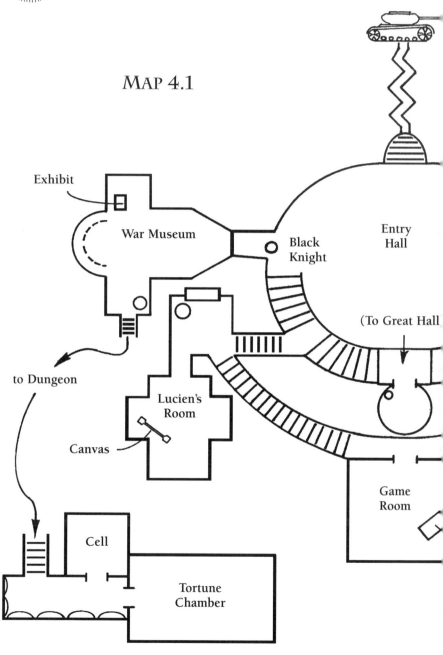

Exhibit

War Museum

Black
Knight

Entry
Hall

to Dungeon

(To Great Hall

Lucien's
Room

Canvas

Game
Room

Cell

Tortune
Chamber

To Desert Complex
(Map 4.2)

CASTLE IRONDUNE

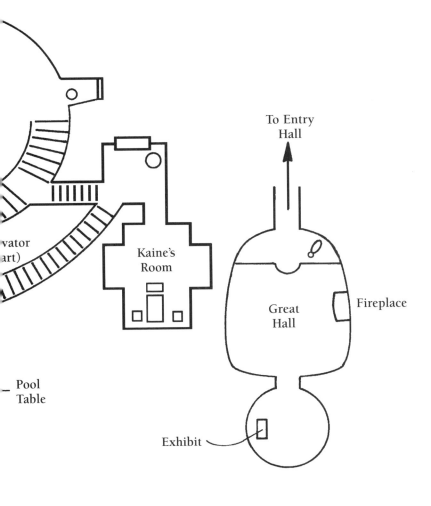

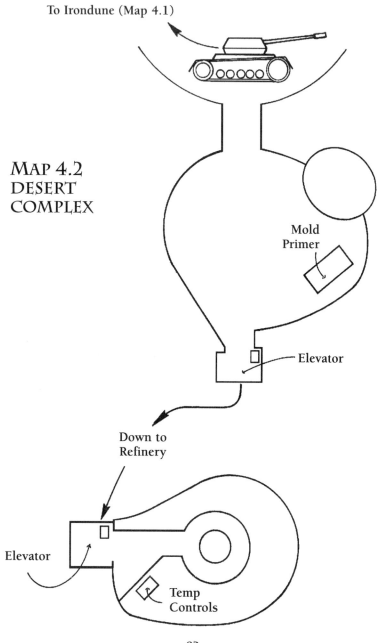

To Irondune (Map 4.1)

MAP 4.2
DESERT
COMPLEX

Mold
Primer

Elevator

Down to
Refinery

Elevator

Temp
Controls

- Go forward to the dog's head and click on its ear to load its mouth with bones.
- Back away and click on the dog's tail. Boom! You've just opened a locked door the easy way.
- Approach the fireplace on the left side of the hall. See the broken sword hanging on the mantle?
- Use the broken hilt on the broken sword.
- Watch the father/son confrontation. When the vision ends, take the sword.
- Exit the hall through the door you just blew open.

WAR ROOM

- View the various simulations, if you want.
- Go to the "Battle In Progress" display (second display on right-hand side).
- Set the number display to match the code for the battle plan you found in Kaine's trunk and Bivotar's journal. That would be Distraction, Build Bridge, Split Troops, Infiltrate, and then Verify Message—10, 1, 9, 6, 12.
- Press the Enter button.
- Irondune is secure! Now you can get out the front door past the old soldier. Unfortunately, you have nowhere to go yet.
- Go back to the entry hall.

ENTRY HALL

- Face the front door, and then turn left.
- Go forward into the alcove and approach the all-black suit

of armor. (If the suit of armor has red sleeves, you're at the wrong suit; cross the hall to the alcove on the other side.)

℮ Put the re-forged sword (from the Great Hall) in the scabbard on the knight's belt.

℮ Turn right and go through the now-open door.

WAR MUSEUM

℮ Whatever you do, don't touch anything in the Age of Kaine exhibit yet. Go to the stained-glass windows of the knights.

℮ Jot a sketch or description of each knight, and note if the visor is up or down.

Remember the odd poem in Kaine's drawer? Five brave fellows stand guard over my dungeon; three are blind, two can see. You must go to each of the five suits of armor in the castle and adjust the visor up or down to match its position in the stained glass depiction. Here's a list:

Knight	Location	Visor
All Black	Entry Hall	Down
Black with red sleeves	Entry Hall	Up
Spiky knees, sword on back	Outside Kaine's Room	Down
Shield, blue helmet plume	Outside Lucien's Room	Up
Multi-color stripes	War Museum	Down

℮ After all five visors are correctly adjusted, a door opens next to the knight in the War Museum. Go through it to the dungeon.

DUNGEON CORRIDOR

- ❦ Follow the dungeon corridor to the open cell on the left.
- ❦ Examine the sketches on the walls, and then exit.
- ❦ Continue down the corridor into the "persuasion" room.

TORTURE CHAMBER

- ❦ What a cheery place this is! Take a tour of the interesting devices, if you can stomach it. All you learn here is what you already know—the radio codes for the battle plan which you've already executed.
- ❦ Exit and go back upstairs to the War Museum.

WAR MUSEUM

- ❦ Go to the Age of Kaine exhibit and look in. Uh-oh, somebody broke the glass.
- ❦ In the close-up, click the red button on the bottle-shaped container to open it.

WARNING! THE FOLLOWING STEPS MUST BE DONE QUICKLY. YOU ARE ABOUT TO HANDLE HIGHLY UNSTABLE THADDIUM.

- Open the black cylinder.
- Take out the radioactive Thaddium capsule and put it in the bottle-shaped container.
- Close the container and pick it up.
- Hurry out of the war museum to the front door of the entry hall.

CASTLE ENTRY

- Click on the front entry door. After the old soldier congratulates you and leaves, follow him through the door.
- Quickly zigzag down the trench to the tank.
- Climb into the tank.

Hurry! The disaster clock is still ticking.

INSIDE TANK

- Once inside, turn left and go to the blue containment vessel just to the left of the axes.
- Open the vessel.
- Put in the Thaddium container.
- Close the vessel. Safe!
- Turn around and approach the tank's control panel.
- Click on the six-digit code entry mechanism on the left side of the panel.

You need to enter a six-digit destination code. Think back. What other six-digit numbers have you seen recently? Aha . . . the pool ball number sequences back in the castle gaming room. But there were four of them. Which one do you want? You could try them all, of course, but think about where you're at. Look out the window. Sand. Dunes. Remember the code for pool shot number 3, which was called "Fishing in the Desert"?

- ℭ Enter the destination code: 7, 4, 1, 9, 5, 3. Exit the close-up.
- ℭ Click on the control joystick (ha, ha) at right.
- ℭ When the tank stops, exit into the desert complex.

DESERT COMPLEX

- ℭ Cross the room to the big black mechanism—the Mold Primer.
- ℭ You need to form the ♂ on the 2 x 2 grid at right. Select the four correct squares from the collection of eight squares in the center of the mechanism. (This is pretty simple.)
- ℭ Click on the handle at far left.
- ℭ Take the mold from the tray just below the eight squares.
- ℭ Turn right and follow the passage into the elevator.

ELEVATOR

- ℭ Another timed puzzle! So move fast. Click on the switch to lower the elevator.
- ℭ When the elevator stops, the disaster clock starts ticking. (You hear the pleasant warning.) Hurry out and into the lab.

KAINE'S PROCESSING LAB

℃ Go to the temperature control panel on the right side of the walkway.

℃ Click the red Reset button to activate the controls.

℃ Click buttons to raise the temperature. You need to get the temperature set right in the middle of the gauge. When you hear a *ding!* the temperature is correct and the iron is at optimal processing consistency. If you overshoot the middle mark, you have to click the Reset button and start over again.

℃ To avoid time-consuming resets, click all four buttons in the middle horizontal row, and then click the two leftmost buttons in the bottom horizontal row. (Listen for that *ding!*)

℃ Turn left and go to the machine at the end of the walkway.

℃ Slide the mold (from the Mold Primer upstairs) into the brown box-like compartment on the left side of the machine.

℃ Click the Arm button. The arm extracts the red-hot molded iron.

℃ Click the Fan button to cool the mold.

℃ Move forward to get a close-up, and then click on the molded iron symbol. You teleport back to the altar in the Temple.

TEMPLE ALTAR

℃ Click on the new elemental symbol. This fills the center receptacle with a blood-red liquid.

- ⟨ Click on the center receptacle and watch the disturbing vision of Kaine's death.
- ⟨ Click on Kaine's glowing sarcophagus to hear his message. He seems to feel genuine remorse for his mistakes. Like the others, he asks you to bring the remaining alchemical metals and help forge the Philosopher's Stone.
- ⟨ Go to the planetarium.

TEMPLE PLANETARIUM

Drag the handle on the right podium counterclockwise until you hear the first ding. This triggers a journey to the Gray Mountains Asylum, workplace of Doctor Erasmus Sartorius.

CHAPTER FIVE

GRAY MOUNTAINS ASYLUM

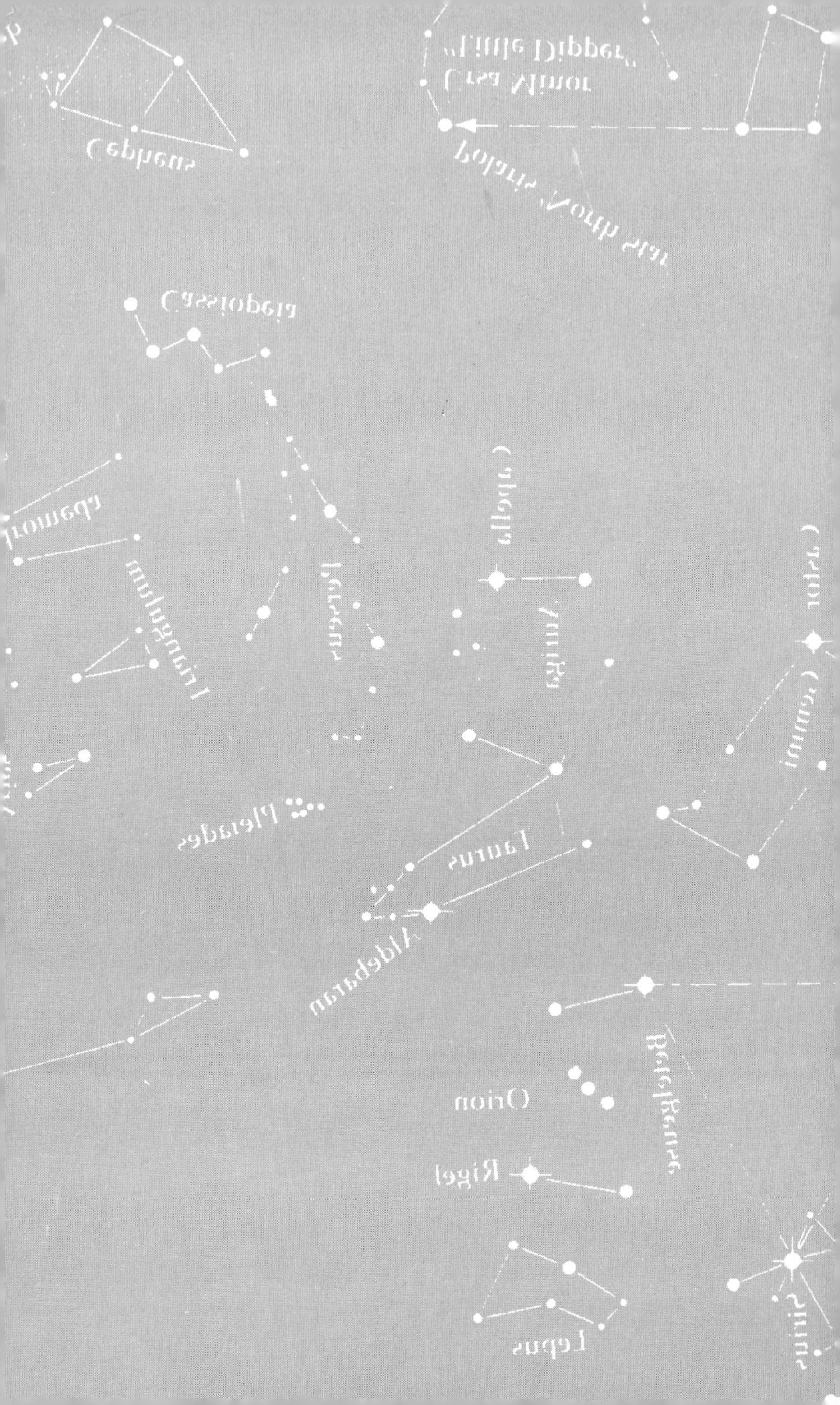

Asylums are creepy places to begin with. Throw in a little Nemesis action and you've got a nut house of the first magnitude. Bivotar's journal calls it "a haunted place." I call it All Hell squared. Unfortunately, you need that elemental metal—in this case, tin. As in the other locations, you arrive on a balcony. Off to one side is the spinning orb of Juperon (Jupiter). You can use the orb to teleport back to the Temple planetarium.

FLOOR 01

- Enter the building and turn left.
- Follow the walkway to the first room on the left.

FILE ROOM

- Read everything you can find in here. Start on the left side at the open file drawer just past the ladder.
- Pull the file on Zoe Wolfe. Holy cow! Could this woman be related to Alexandria?
- Search the left wall until you find a drawer with the corner of a file poking out. (It's in the second vertical column from the end.) Click on it to pull it open.
- Open the file on Malveaux and read his letters to Dr. Sartorius.
- Turn toward the table and click on the flashlight. When it shines in your eyes, click on it again. Watch the vision of Sartorius examining Zoe Wolfe.
- Turn around to face the door, and then go to the file drawer just past the ladder on the left.
- Read the file on Lucien Kaine.
- Don't miss the file on Leon Mason, tucked right behind Lucien's. What a head case!
- Move toward the door and open the file drawer three columns to the right of the drawer with Lucien's file. Examine the colorful doodles of "Patient X." Note the fairly cogent comment: "Helium injection should empty excess liquid."
- Exit the room and turn left.
- Follow the walkway to the next room on the left.

CRANIAL LABORATORY

- ❦ Now here's a room where you can really get ahead in this game. Go forward to the table and examine the collection.

- ❦ Note the electrical device with five buttons. What do you suppose goes on that spike? Wait, I've got it. *A head!* (I don't know where I got the idea.)

- ❦ Turn left and go to the x-ray machine. Let's fool around with it for awhile.

- ❦ Push the A button. The mechanical arm picks up one of the canisters on the right and puts it in the receptacle box—the box where the x-ray gun is pointing, just left of the gauge.

- ❦ Pull the handle on the box. This activates the x-ray gun.

- ❦ Click on the blue glowing box for an x-ray peek into the guts of the canister.

- ❦ Move back, pull the handle again, and click on the R button. The mechanical arm puts the canister in the slot. The canister disappears.

You can repeat this process forever, if you want. Nothing will be accomplished, and don't expect me to wait around for you.

- ❦ Here's an idea: Click the A button again, but this time click on the receptacle box for a close-up, and then take the canister.

- ❦ Go to the device on the other side of the room.

- ❦ What the heck is it? Don't ask me. I'm just a cheat book. Do I look like I know everything? Well, OK . . . put the canister into the clamps at the top.

Notice how the device pours the red glop into the bowl, and then distills it away to nothingness. Neat!

ℭ Cross the room to that freezer in the corner.

ℭ Open the freezer, look in, and take the small safe.

ℭ Go back to the x-ray machine and click on the receptacle box.

ℭ In the close-up, put the safe (from the freezer) into the box.

ℭ Click on the top of the safe to get a top view. Twiddle the dial a bit if you want, but clearly, you need a combination to open the thing. Do you have one? I think not.

ℭ Move back twice, then pull the handle on the front of the machine.

ℭ Go forward to the now-blue box for an x-ray close-up of the safe—hey, there's a key in there! And the last two numbers of the combination are visible, too—20 and 18.

ℭ Exit the close-up of the x-ray machine. (Don't worry, we can just leave the safe.)

ℭ Exit the room and turn left.

ℭ Follow the walkway to the elevator on the left.

ELEVATOR

ℭ Enter and click on the right-hand control panel for a close-up.

ℭ Push the "close doors" button.

ℭ Now go to the destination control panel in the other corner.

ℭ Click on the "B" key to turn it and ride down to the basement.

ℭ When you arrive, push the "open doors" button and exit.

MORGUE

- ℂ Ah, breathe in that fresh air!
- ℂ Go down to the end of the room and examine that box-and-bowl thing.

The box looks to be about one body-length long. And that bowl's big enough to hold, I don't know, a human head or something. Man, who splattered all that red paint everywhere?

- ℂ Go back to the control handles and mess with them for a while.

Some quick experimentation reveals that the left handle raises the box, and the middle handle moves the bowl under the hole in the box (a hole placed conveniently where one's head might be if one were to lay in the box, which one would never do, would one?). The right handle drops the guillotine blade through the box, lowers the bowl, and flips the box up to dispose of whatever it is that might be laying in the box.

- ℂ OK, let's check out the drawers. I hate to say this, but you'll find a whole body (with head) somewhere on the right side. To be more specific, go down to the end of the room, turn right to the fourth column of drawers from the left, and look in the third drawer from the bottom.
- ℂ Take the body and turn to the guillotine box.
- ℂ Put the body in the guillotine box. Are you getting sick? I am.
- ℂ Go back to the control handles.
- ℂ Click on the left handle.
- ℂ Click on the middle handle.
- ℂ Click on the right handle.

℃ Go to the bowl and get the head. What the hell, he was dead anyhow.

℃ Get in the elevator, close the doors, and turn the key for Floor 01.

℃ When you arrive, go back to the head shop . . . I mean, the cranial lab.

CRANIAL LAB

℃ I highly recommend that you click all five buttons for some amusing give and take with the "patient." But those of you without patience should click the lower left button and listen to his "little secret"—the number sequence, 36–24–36.

℃ Go to the safe you left in the x-ray machine and enter the combination—36, 24, 36, 20, 18—by clicking on each number on the dial.

℃ When the safe opens, take out the canister.

℃ Take the canister across the room to the distillation device and put it in the holding clamps.

℃ When the distillation is finished, click on the bowl.

℃ Take the key. Say . . . you don't suppose that's an *elevator* key, do you?

℃ Exit the lab and go to the elevator.

ELEVATOR

℃ Get in and close the doors.

℃ Put the new key in slot 20.

- ℂ Click on the key to turn it. Ride up to 20th floor.
- ℂ When you arrive, open the doors and exit.
- ℂ Turn right and go to the first door on the right.

"WOBBLY" DOOR

- ℂ Hmmm. Something about that door is very strange. And it won't open. Let's move on.
- ℂ Continue down the walkway to the next door.

THERAPY ROOM

- ℂ Wow. It's the Chair from Gynecology Hell. Sit in it. Nothing happens . . . yet.
- ℂ Get up, turn right, and go to the table with the microscopes.
- ℂ Look in the microscopes. (Parents, cover the eyes of your kids first. There's *sex* going on in there.)
- ℂ Click on the books for a close-up.
- ℂ Read the excerpt from *The Embryo: Mystical Conception and Creation*. Most interesting.
- ℂ Turn around and click on the bloody examination table.
- ℂ Click on the syringe and watch the not-so-mystical conception of Alexandria Wolfe.
- ℂ Now try to cross the room.

Meet "Doctor Sartorius." You can do what she says: Sit down in the chair. Or you can keep clicking on the far doorway for awhile and see what she does. It's kind of fun.

GRAY MOUNTAINS ASYLUM

MAP 5

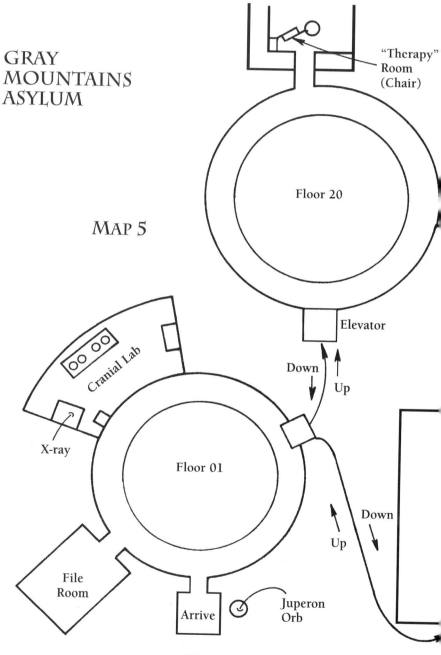

"Therapy" Room (Chair)

Floor 20

Elevator

Down

Up

Cranial Lab

X-ray

Floor 01

Down

Up

File Room

Arrive

Juperon Orb

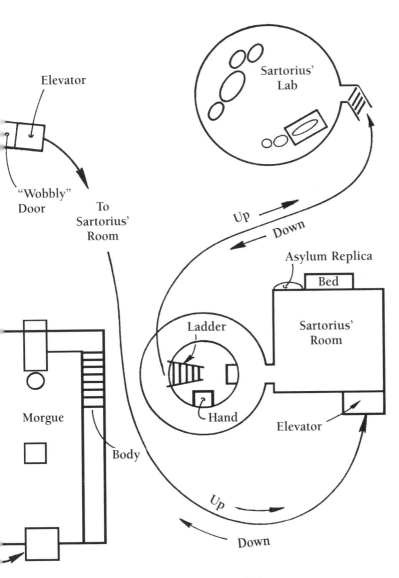

Sartorius'
Lab

Elevator

"Wobbly"
Door

To
Sartorius'
Room

Up

Down

Asylum Replica

Bed

Ladder

Sartorius'
Room

Hand

Morgue

Body

Elevator

Up

Down

- (Sit down in the chair. It's looking-glass time!
- (The effect won't last long. Exit the room quickly and go back to the wobbly door.

"WOBBLY" DOOR

- (While you wobble, click on the door to open it. An elevator!
- (Click the Up button. The elevator rises one floor to the private room of Dr. Sartorius.

SARTORIUS' ROOM

- (Take two steps forward and turn right.
- (Read the journal of Sartorius.

Note the good doctor's growing obsession with alchemy, the Philosopher's Stone, and "perfect knowledge." Note his arrogance and disregard for the other alchemists and their "mundane reasons." The last entry is particularly disturbing. Apparently, Sartorius sees perfect, purely distilled blood—"the essence of innocence"—as the key to the fifth element, the Quintessence.

- (Turn left and go to the display straight ahead.
- (Read the letters to Sartorius from the Enchanters Guild and Sophia Hamilton.

Clearly, the doctor was under pressure from all sides, giving him plenty of motivation to accelerate the pace of his research. His own letter to one Dr. Frobbian displays his impatience. But the question arises: Does Sartorius truly seek to defend his patients, the "forgotten waifs" he mentions? Or is all this concern a cover for his true obsession, the lifelong search for the Philosopher's Stone begun by his father? I'm inclined to cut him some slack, but that's the kind of guy I am. Cynics may see a more bloody underlying purpose to all this cranial research and such.

- Turn around and step to the center of the room.
- Turn back and approach the bed chamber (the big alcove in the middle).
- Click on the box and take the reflex mallet.
- Back away from the bed chamber and go to the next display to the left, the replica of the asylum.
- Click on the base of the replica. Hear that sound? You just activated something that you'll need later.
- Face away from the replica and go to the next display on the right.
- Read the book lying flat.

Note in particular how the miniature opera hall worked "as a kind of central control for the greater structure itself." Didn't you just click something on the asylum replica? Do you wonder what you activated? If you go out right now and buy copies of this book for everyone you know, I'll give you the answer.

- Read the excerpts from *The Blood Alchemist* by the father of our Doctor Sartorius. Note the written inscription from old Lew.
- Aha! So the Temple altar is a shrine which has the power to create the Philosopher's Stone. Now turn the page and pay *very close attention* to Table 12g (right page), which delineates the purification process for tin. Fluorine must be present in the atmosphere. Helium "raises." Oxygen alone "is without effect." (So why mention it in the process? Hmmm.) And hydrogen and oxygen burn coolly to create water . . .

⦅ Exit the close-up of the book display.

⦅ Go through the doorway to the left of the display.

ANATOMY ROOM

Don't touch the electrical box yet! If you do, you will expire in a most expeditious fashion. Instead, look around a bit. The doc sure loves those body parts, doesn't he? Explore the room, pushing buttons.

⦅ When you get to the hand display, break the glass with the reflex mallet.

⦅ Take the hand.

⦅ Go to the electrical box and use the hand on it.

⦅ When the door opens, climb the ladder up to the laboratory. If the ladder is not down, see the note just below.

DID YOU BUY THOSE EXTRA COPIES OF THIS BOOK FOR YOUR FRIENDS? WELL, OK, I'LL TELL YOU ANYWAY. THE ASYLUM REPLICA BACK IN SARTORIUS' ROOM CONTROLS THIS LADDER. IF YOU DIDN'T CLICK ON THE BASE OF THE REPLICA LIKE I TOLD YOU TO, THE LADDER DIDN'T LOWER.

SARTORIUS' LABORATORY

  ❧ Cool stuff! First, go to the basin area to the left.

  ❧ Examine the two big battery-like things to the right of the basin.

Note that the red light is on, indicating inactivity. Note also that tubes run from the basin through the batteries, then wires run from the batteries to the device across the room. Apparently, these batteries power the device. (I can't be sure, of course. This is an *unauthorized* guide.)

  ❧ Examine the basin.

  ❧ Click on the spigot over the center of the basin. This fills the basin with a liquid.

  ❧ Click on the handle at the back right of the basin. This drains the liquid into the batteries and triggers a throbbing sound.

  ❧ Look at the batteries again. Green lights on. Powered up!

  ❧ Go to the glass globe. Does that look like a big hunk of tin in there? (It should, because it is.)

Remember the purification process from *The Blood Alchemist* back in Sartorius' room? Note that a tank of helium is connected to the globe at left; tanks of oxygen and hydrogen run into the globe from the right side. Recall that these are all part of the purification process for tin. The first thing that we need to do is melt down that hunk of tin.

  ❧ Click on the pair of tanks at right.

THE GAME IS VERY FORGIVING IF YOU SCREW UP THE ORDER OF STEPS HERE, SO DON'T WORRY ABOUT SAVING YOUR GAME AFTER EVERY STEP.

Note the valves at the top of each tank—left is off, right is on. So the oxygen is on, the hydrogen off. But remember—"oxygen alone is without effect." So let's shoot some hydrogen into the globe and see what happens.

- Move the hydrogen valve to the right to turn it on.
- Move the oxygen valve to the left to turn it off. The globe is now full of a highly combustible hydrogen.
- Step back and pull the switch to the right of the globe.

The metal melts and pours into a mold. Now you need to cool it. Where can you find some water? (Hint: Water is H2O.) Again, remember *The Blood Alchemist*—oxygen and hydrogen together "burn coolly" to form water.

- Go to the oxygen tank and turn it on by flipping the valve to the right.

❦ Step back and pull the switch again. The water cools the pure metal, which raises from the mold.

Last step coming up. Remember that "helium raises." Also think back to the colorful note in the file of Patient X down in the File Room: "Helium injection should empty excess liquid."

❦ Click on the helium tank.

❦ After the globe raises, move forward to get a close-up, and then click on the molded tin symbol. You teleport back to the altar in the Temple.

CHAPTER SIX

ENDGAME

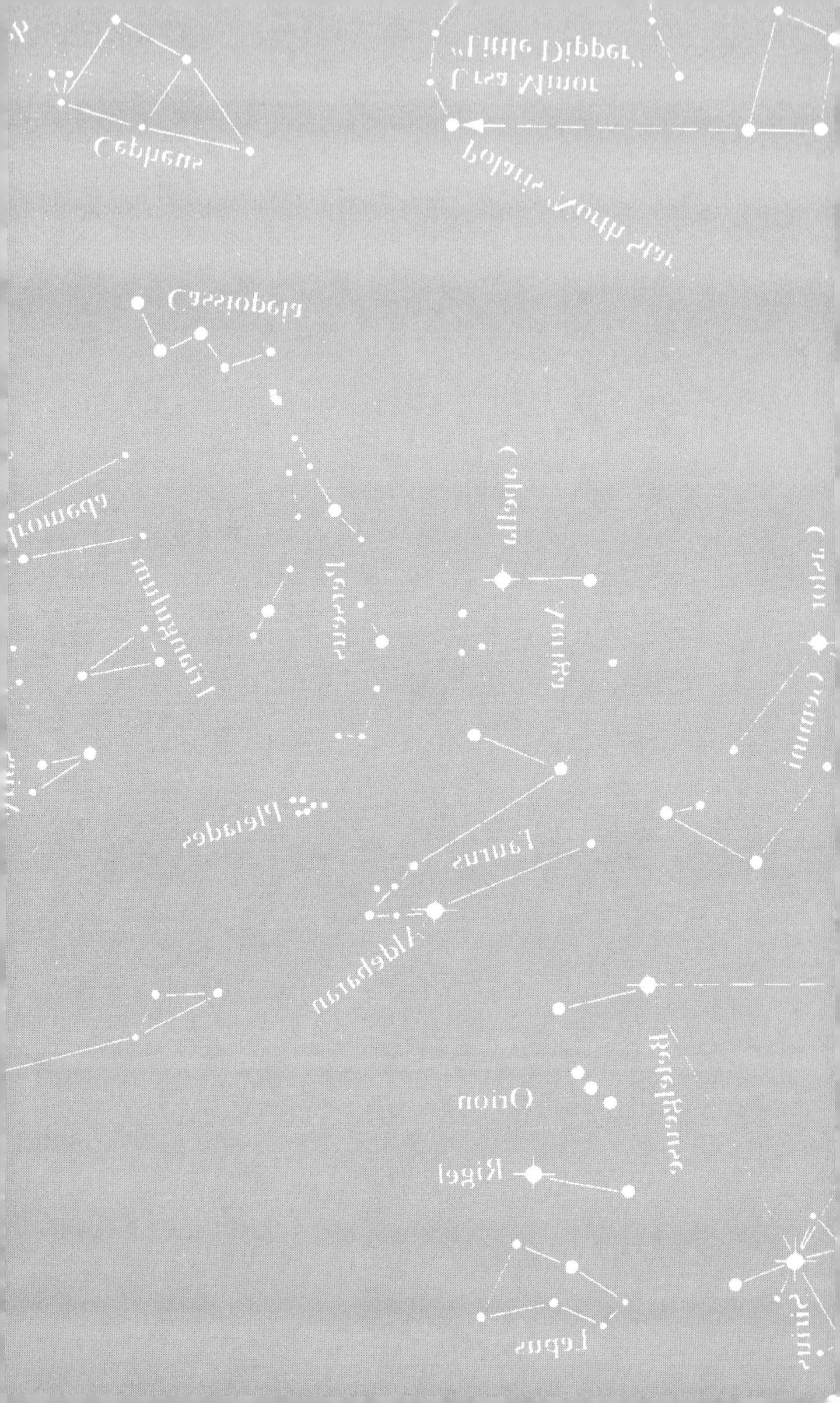

Cepheus

"Little Dipper"
(Ursa Minor)

the two north pointer stars

Cassiopeia

Andromeda

Triangulum

Perseus

Capella

Auriga

Canis Minor

Pleiades

Taurus

Aldebaran

Betelgeuse

Orion

Rigel

Lepus

Sirius

he alchemists gather around the altar. What a nice bunch of people! They are most gratified that you have liberated them. They offer you the elixir of life, and they beg you to drink it before they all perish.

TEMPLE ALTAR

⟨ *Don't drink the cup!* Wait until the cup explodes.

⟨ Then watch the scene unfold.

The alchemists show their true colors. They want immortality, and they're willing to use Alexandria's blood—her "spirit," according to the giggling Sartorius—to get it. Fortunately, they have no more use for you. After summoning the so-called Nemesis, they turn to invoke the Great Eclipse. After poor Lucien tosses you the ring, you end up in the fountain atrium of the Temple.

FOUNTAIN ATRIUM

⟨ Click on the ring to take it—and see a horrifying vision of the blood ritual.

⟨ Turn right and step forward to the fountains.

⟨ Turn to face the fountain on the left.

⟨ Click on the right-hand horn to stop the water flow.

⟨ Go forward for a close-up of the skeletal hand.

⟨ Click the ring on the hand. Down we go!

UNDERGROUND TEMPLE (ANTECHAMBER)

⟨ Take one step forward, turn right, and read the inscription on the tablet. All you need is love! Isn't that sweet? It's so good to know that the Beatles were right.

⟨ Exit the close-up, and turn left and approach the portal.

UNDERGROUND CHAMBER

- Go around to the other side of the tomb in the center of the room and approach it for a close-up.
- Click on the tomb to see a vision of Alexandria. She leaves a silver ring on the tomb.
- Click Lucien's gold ring on the silver ring. You now have both rings.
- Approach that toothy dragon statue on the opposite side of the room.
- Put the rings in the basin before it.
- Click on the triangle to the right of the dragon.
- After the dragon melts the rings, take the bowl of melted metal from the basin.
- Approach the elephant statue.
- Put the bowl in the basin before the elephant.
- Click on the triangle to the right of the elephant.
- After the elephant cools the metal, take the warm lump of malleable metal from the basin.
- Approach the snake statue.
- Put the lump of metal in the mold before the statue.
- Click on the triangle to the right of the snake.
- After the snake presses the mold, take the molded metal from the basin.
- Approach the strange demon holding the glass globe.
- Place the molded metal on the platform in front of him.

I bet you jumped ahead of me and clicked on the triangle to the right of the demon, didn't you? And nothing happened. And then you clicked on the demon's outstretched hand and discovered a cursor change, indicating that you need something else to put there. What is it?

- ₡ Step back from the demon statue and go toward the elephant statue.
- ₡ Turn to look at the tomb in the center of the room.
- ₡ Move the cursor to the top of the screen and click when you see the forward arrow.
- ₡ Grab the scepter that falls.
- ₡ Take the scepter back to the demon statue and put it in the outstretched hand.
- ₡ After the demon purifies the double-ring metal, take it. You transport to a walkway overlooking the Temple altar.

TEMPLE WALKWAY

- ₡ Turn left and look down at the altar.
- ₡ Don't be a loser! Click the double-ring on the rising body . . . and watch the game-ending movie.

One more thing: After Alexandria and Lucien walk off (into the sunset, I presume), step back, turn around, go through the cemetery gate, and swivel to see the Venus painting. Click on it for . . . final credits!

APPENDIX

RETURN TO ZORK

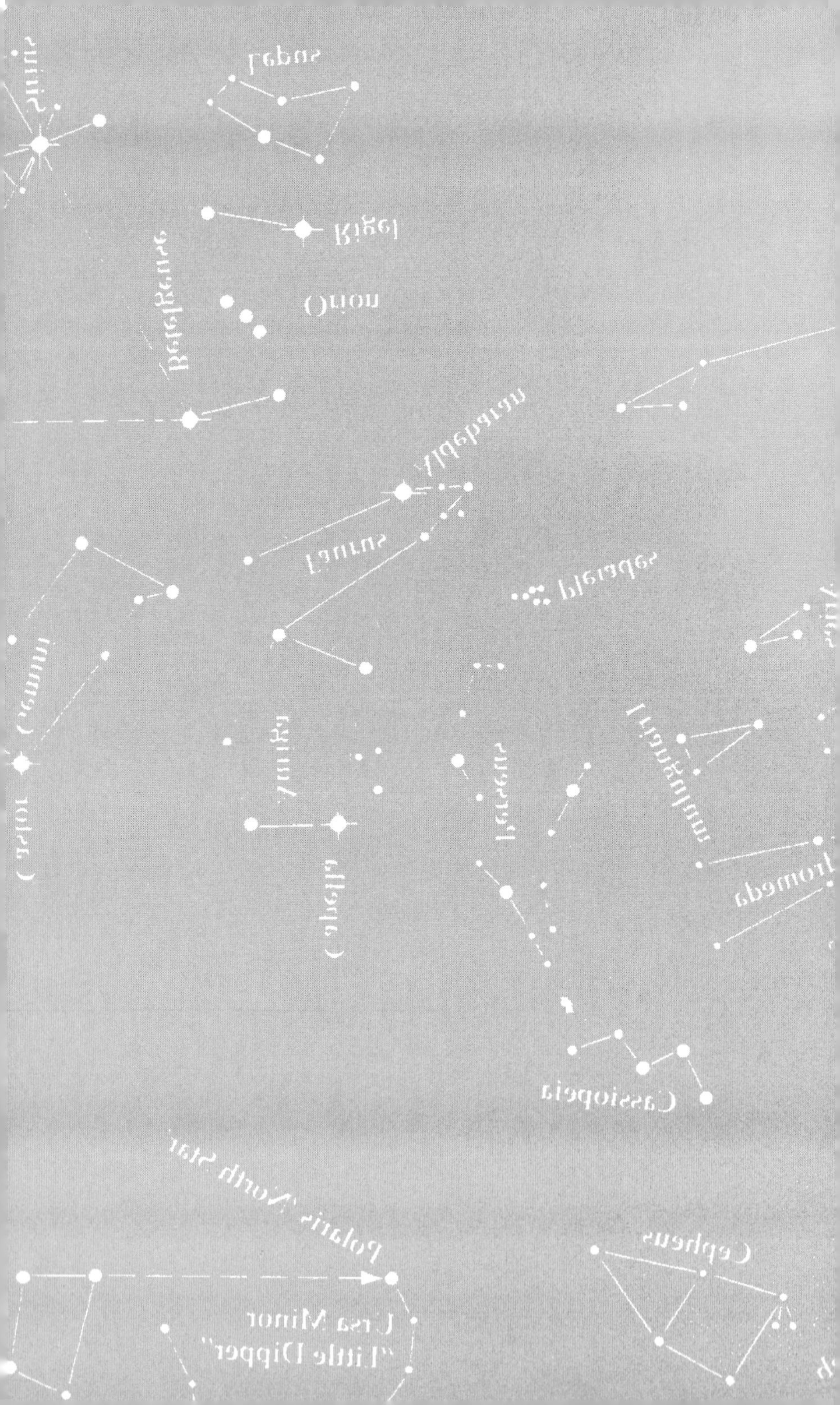

lthough the old Zork Infocom games were text-only adventures, the immediate predecessor of *Zork Nemesis* is a multimedia treat in its own right. Measured by 1994 standards, *Return to Zork* is very nearly a perfect game. It's amusing, clever, beautiful, challenging, and it all adds up to a perfect 10 in the overall fun category. Several industry magazines selected *Return to Zork* as Game of the Year two years ago, and it still holds up well against all the new techno-marvels of 1996. I probably had more raw fun playing *Return to Zork* than any other title in the past few years.

THE STORY

Here's the *Return to Zork* premise. You are you, and you've just won the Grand Prize in a Vacation Sweepstakes. The prize package features an all-expenses-paid, four-day stay in some resort called "the fabulous Valley of the Sparrows." You receive this information via an amusing letter packed into the *Return to Zork* game box.

But when you arrive in the fabulous valley, you find the "Sparrows" in the name has been summarily replaced by "Vultures." Before long, you're wandering amongst the ruins of the lost Underground Empire of Zork, a legendary world hidden away 400 years ago during something called the Great Diffusion. You quickly learn that an evil magic power embodied in someone named Morphius has re-inhabited the land . . . and of course it's up to you to reign in the guy.

Your adventure actually starts above ground. After a little white-water rafting you end up in the forlorn little town of West Shanbar, where the mayor's a hustler, the mill owner's a lush, and the schoolmarm's a . . . well, a schoolmarm. A little exploring leads you underground.

Your ultimate objective is to gather all six pieces of the mythical Flying Disc of Frobozz so that you may fling it at the Wall of Illusion and face Morphius himself in a life-or-death game of modified chess called Survivor.

GENERAL TIPS

USE YOUR TOOLS!

Use your camera to photograph everybody in Zork who seems in any way important. Your photo album will elicit a *lot* of useful information from characters you meet. The same is true of the notebook you get from Ms. Peepers (*if* you pass her quiz.) All the pertinent information that you learn on your journey is automatically recorded there. Refer to it whenever you find yourself stuck.

Killing Is Bad . . . Unless It's Good, of Course

Look, this isn't an FRP. You can't just hack and slash your way to victory in Zork. These people have *rules* here. Mindless violence and sundry other felonious acts will often be punished. You could even lose your inventory. However, a sly burglary or a good whack upside the head isn't *always* a bad thing. Just keep in mind that antisocial activities, when called for, will appear to be fairly obvious courses of action.

Ask Everybody Everything

When you meet a new Zorkian (Zorkoid, Zorker, whatever) click on the Ask icon (the question mark) then click on every other icon that appears. Also, if you meet the same character later, ask them everything again—there may be new information lurking in that vertical icon stack.

THE FLY-THROUGH

1. Approach to Shanbar

MOUNTAIN PASS

Pick up the rock and throw it at the vulture. Zoom in on the sign. Use your knife to dig up the bonding plant. Go forward.

LIGHTHOUSE

Enter the Lighthouse. Talk to the Lighthouse keeper. For fun, ask him about the map and click on the road to the south to get the his reaction.

BEHIND THE LIGHTHOUSE

Use the knife to cut the vines. Tie the vines to the planks to form a raft. Ride the raft downstream.

RIVER

When the bridge appears, you will automatically exit to the left. (You have to do this manually in the disk-based version of the game.)

2. WEST SHANBAR

MAYOR'S OFFICE (TOWN HALL)

The first building on the right is the town hall. Optional: Browse through the files for some quite useful information.

SCHOOLHOUSE

The first building on the right is the schoolhouse. Use the knife or some other solid object to ring the bell outside the schoolhouse. Ms. Peepers will let you in.

QUIZ

Answer Ms. Peepers' question. (All answers are in the Encyclopedia Frobozzica that accompanies the game.) If you answer correctly, she'll give you a notebook. Use this to record pertinent info as you travel through Zork.

GIFT SHOP (FIRST VISIT)

The second building on the left is the gift shop. The door is locked. You cannot enter yet.

HARDWARE STORE

The second building on the right is the hardware store. Pick up the crank and box, then place them in your inventory. The mice are worthless, game-wise. If you want, you can pick them up—but be sure to put them into the box to avoid catching hantavirus.

THE BRIDGE

Go back to the town entrance. Turn around to face the bridge. Click to the right of the bridge (down arrow) to visit the waif under the bridge.

UNDER THE BRIDGE (FIRST VISIT)

Talk to the waif. He'll offer information, but nothing more yet. (Don't get tough or show him anything scary; he'll run away.) Go back up to the bridge, then go left to the Old Mill.

OLD MILL (FIRST VISIT)

Drink with Boos Myller, the drunken operator of the mill. Each time he fills your glass, dump it into the plant, then offer a toast. When Boos recites the correct line from the Shanbar toasting ritual, drink from the empty glass. After the third toast, ask for his keys. Ask any further questions before the fourth toast is complete. (You *can* come back later, when he's sober.)

When Boos passes out after the fourth toast, put his silver flask into your inventory. (Note the trap door.) Now go through the door on the left to get behind the Old Mill. Retrieve the key and flip the chock to activate the water wheel. (If the trap door didn't appear when Boos passed out, it will now.) Go to the gift shop.

GIFT SHOP (SECOND VISIT)

Use the single key (from behind the Old Mill) to open the door to the Gift Shop. Take the battery and place it into the Tele-Orb. Zoom in on the cash register to open it. Take the tickets and coins. Go back to visit the waif under the bridge.

UNDER THE BRIDGE (SECOND VISIT)

Give the Dizzyland/Dizzyworld tickets to the waif. He'll give you a gift in return. Go back to the old mill.

OLD MILL (SECOND VISIT)

Go down through the trap door. Use Boos' set of keys to open the door at the bottom, and enter the New Mill, which is a portal to the underground.

3. EAST SHANBAR (UNDERGROUND VILLAGE)

NEW MILL

From the door, go left to East Shanbar. The path on the right leads to the Hero's Memorial.

GENERAL STORE

The first building on the left is the general store. You can't unlock the door here yet. Keep going.

MOODOCK'S ARMORY

Play Survivor with Moodock. If you win, he'll give you a coin and a rusty old sword.

BLACKSMITH SHOP (FIRST VISIT)

Give the blacksmith your old sword.

INN OF ISENOUGH

Talk to Molly to get information. You can't check into a room yet.

BLACKSMITH SHOP (SECOND VISIT)

Pay the blacksmith for repairing your sword. If you show the blacksmith the sword and then threaten him, he will exchange it for the Dwarven Sword. (If you accept the first sword he gives you, you'll have to return when it shatters.) Go back to the bridge and turn left to the boat dock.

BOAT DOCK (FIRST VISIT)

Click on the knot Ben is tying. He'll teach you the cow hitch. Show Ben a photo of any woman or play him a recording of a woman's voice. He'll give you a letter for Witch Itah. Now cross the bridge into New West Shanbar.

4. NEW WEST SHANBAR

HERO'S MEMORIAL

Nothing of interest here. Turn left to the Fool's Memorial.

FOOL'S MEMORIAL

Take the book from the base of the memorial. (When you first meet Rebecca on the road, show her this book. She won't be able to translate it then, but she will the next time you find her.) Continue down the road to Snoot's farm.

SNOOT'S FARM

Climb in the window of Rebecca's trailer. Enter her bathroom, the door is on the back wall; she's a real knockout. When you awake, she'll give you another quiz. Again, the answer is in the Encyclopedia

Frobozzica. Now go through the door on the right into the bedroom. Take the mirror. Try to enter the other bedroom, then make Alexis snarl at you—you'll need the recording later—then head for the kitchen.

In the kitchen, open the refrigerator and take the meat. Take the thermozz from the table. Pick up the soap, drop it in the sink, and turn on the water. Wash the waif's gift in the soapy water. Exit the trailer.

To the right of the trailer is the silo. Insert the crank into the silo latch and turn it clockwise. Add carrots to your inventory. Go back to face the Fool's Memorial, then go right to Pugney's ranch.

PUGNEY'S RANCH

Pugney's house is the building on the right. Tap on the window and talk to Pugney. Be apologetic; you'll get permission to take the bra box out on the lawn. Ask him about the book; he'll translate the

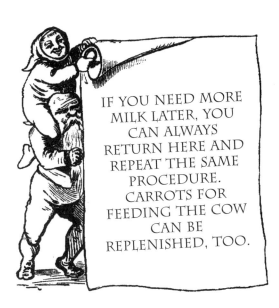

IF YOU NEED MORE MILK LATER, YOU CAN ALWAYS RETURN HERE AND REPEAT THE SAME PROCEDURE. CARROTS FOR FEEDING THE COW CAN BE REPLENISHED, TOO.

title for you. Back away, take the bra box, back away again, and go into the barn (the building on the left).

You'll soon notice that the meat is rotting. Pick up the hay, then drop or throw it. Light a match and use it to burn the hay. Warm your hands over the hay. Pick up the thermozz and use it to catch the milk as you milk the cow. Since you just burned the cow's food, feed your carrots to the hungry animal.

Now go back through East Shanbar, then take the left fork in the road to the ruins.

5. OUTSIDE EAST SHANBAR

RUINS

Pick up the tiles. Turn around to see more of the ruins. Put the tiles in the frame on the ground, then examine the frame to see the puzzle. No cheat here—you have to solve the sliding tile puzzle on your own. When the puzzle is completed, it reads: "Water unseen at falls mix with bat dropping yields potion for invisibility." The lower text reads: " . . . Search for three more pieces on the ground where this was found." On the ground you'll find another disc piece and two illumynite rocks. Put them in your inventory. Continue on down the path to the Forest of the Spirits.

FOREST OF THE SPIRITS

Go to the Coin Tree (with metal leaves). Use your sword to strike the tree, then pick up the zorkmids that fall to the ground.

Find the Bowman. To cure his blindness, give him the thermozz of milk. He'll give you his bow and arrows. Go to the Fairy's location and strike a match to avoid a Grue attack. When the Fairy appears, give a friendly reaction. She'll give you a bag of fairy dust.

Find the Tree Spirit and listen to her songs, which change with your reaction to her. Now find the Pile of Leaves. Throw something

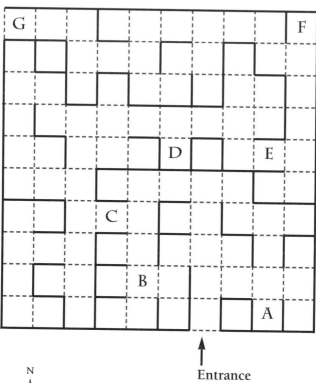

Entrance

N
W — E
S

Key
A = Coin tree
B = Bowman
C = Fairy
D = Tree Spirit
E = Leaf trap
F = Boar statue
G = Giant spider

WHENEVER YOU'RE SHORT ON CASH, COME BACK TO THE FOREST FOR MORE ZORKMIDS.

(but not your sword) at them to spring the trap, then use your sword to free whatever you just threw. Strike the Hungry Boar Memorial three times with your sword, then take the third disc piece. Avoid the Giant Spider for now. Retrace your route to the entrance of the forest, then leave.

6. RETURN TO EAST SHANBAR

BLACKSMITH SHOP (SECOND VISIT)

Show the book to the blacksmith. For a fee of two zorkmids, he'll translate a joke. (Don't forget to pick up the rebate of one zorkmid that he returns after smudging your book.)

INN OF ISENOUGH

Go to the Inn and give coins to Molly to pay for a room. Back away from her and click on the elevator. In the room: If the silver flask is empty, fill it with water from the sink—i.e., pick up the flask, click it on the sink, turn on the sink, than quickly click the flask on the sink while the water runs.

Put the illumynite on the nightstand. Zoom in on the monitor; for fun, zoom in on the monitor and watch the commercial. Now turn off the lights. Morphius will enter your dreams. Turn on the lights and retrieve the illumynite.

INCINERATOR

Flip lever #1 to open the incinerator. Throw the bra box over the incinerator wall (click near the top of the screen). Click lever #1 again to close the incinerator, then click lever #2. When the drawer pops open, zoom in and pour water from the flask onto the red-hot wire, then pick up the wire.

GENERAL STORE

Use the wire to pick the lock on the door of the General Store. Shake the cereal box twice to reveal the whistle inside. Take the whistle. Take the mice out of the box and drop them. Pick up the rats and put them in the box. (If you put the rats in before removing the mice, they'll catch the hantavirus and die.)

7. THE WITCH AND THE BOG

BOAT DOCK (SECOND VISIT)

Pay Ben to get a boat. Put a rat into the boat's motor. The boat will take you to the Witch's Hut.

WITCH'S HUT (FIRST VISIT)

Leave the rotting meat outside. When Witch Itah appears, show her the joke book, orb, and thermozz. After you hand her Ben's letter—be sure you haven't opened it!—she'll give you her walking stick for navigating the bogs. Retrieve the meat.

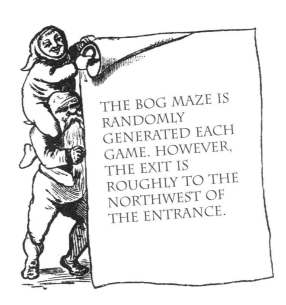

THE BOG MAZE IS RANDOMLY GENERATED EACH GAME. HOWEVER, THE EXIT IS ROUGHLY TO THE NORTHWEST OF THE ENTRANCE.

CREEPING BOGS

Test *every* patch of bog with the witch's stick. (If the stick sinks, so will you if you step on the patch.) When you exit, you'll be at the Whispering Woods.

When you exit, go forward through East Shanbar, then back to the Forest of the Spirits.

FOREST OF THE SPIRITS (SECOND VISIT)

You're probably low on cash at this point. Whack the Coin Tree a few times with your sword. Take the money that falls and return to the Boat Dock.

BOAT DOCK (THIRD VISIT)

Give Ben some zorkmids to get the boat again. It'll take you to the Witch's hut again.

WITCH'S HUT (SECOND VISIT)

Again, leave the rotting meat outside. Ask Witch Itah about the Whispering Woods by pointing to it on the map. Take her bats, retrieve the meat, and go back through the hut to the bogs. (Use the witch's stick again to test each step.)

Now go forward through East Shanbar again, across the bridge to New West Shanbar back to Pugney's ranch. Go past the barn to the left to the Vulture Pits.

8. THE WIZARD'S SHACK

VULTURE PITS

Before entering the pits, sprinkle fairy dust on the rotting meat, then throw the meat. The vultures will eat it and fall asleep. Enter the pit and take the talon.

INN OF ISENOUGH

Return for a nap. (You'll need to give Molly some zorkmids for the room again.) Be sure to put the illumynite on the nightstand and turn off the lights, so Morphius will appear in your dreams again.

REBECCA AND THE MAYOR

When you meet Rebecca on the road, show her the joke book again. She may (or may not) translate a joke. If she won't, go show the book to Ms. Peepers in the schoolhouse. Return to the Mayor's office and show him the book too.

WHISPERING WOODS (FIRST VISIT)

The longer you roam, the dimmer things get. Be sure the thermozz is full of milk before you start. Release the bats. Follow their trail of glowing guano to the exit. Be sure to pick up a sample of the guano for your inventory.

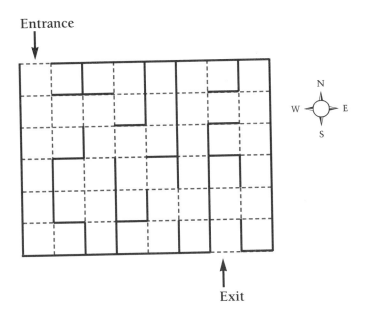

IF YOU GET TEXT THAT MENTIONS THE "MILKY WAY," DRINK SOME MILK TO RESTORE YOUR VISION

FERRYMAN'S DOCK (FIRST VISIT)

Ring the bell three times. Show (do *not* give) the coin you got from Moodock to the ferryman. He'll take you for a ride to Ferryman's Isle.

FERRYMAN'S ISLE

Walk up the path on the left to reach Canuck's Shack.

CANUCK'S SHACK

Enter the shack and examine the blueprints. For fun, feed the scroll to the duck. Toss the resulting egg at the duck. The scroll reappears! OK, now read the scroll to the duck. React in any way except Threaten. (If you do, you'll be turned into a duck, too.) Show Canuck the joke book. When you ask about the bottle, Canuck shrinks you and stuffs you inside.

INSIDE CANUCK'S BOTTLE

Your time is limited, so hurry. Use the combination written on the ship's sail—9427—to open the safe. Remove the disc piece (the fourth one you've found now) and place it in your inventory. Polish the old piece of metal with the rag. Be sure you're holding either the polished metal or the mirror when you leave the bottle so you can reflect Canuck's duck spell when you emerge.

When you exit the shack, the scroll and bottle will automatically pop out of your inventory and back into the shack. Pry open the knocker with your sword; you'll find the magnet. Return to the ferryman's dock.

FERRYMAN'S DOCK (SECOND VISIT)

Ring the bell twice to summon the ferryman for your return trip. Again, just show him the old coin.

WHISPERING WOODS (SECOND VISIT)

To return to East Shanbar, you can follow the guano trail (or your map). But it's easier to use the vulture whistle in combination with the magnet to go to any spot on the map that you choose.

THE WHISTLE AND MAGNET WILL DISAPPEAR FROM YOUR INVENTORY. BUT FROM NOW ON, YOU CAN GO ANYWHERE ON THE MAP BY SIMPLY CLICKING ON THE SPOT YOU WANT.

INN OF ISENOUGH

Rent another room, put the illumynite on the nightstand, turn off the lights, and watch your third Morphius dream.

9. Chuckles Comedy Club

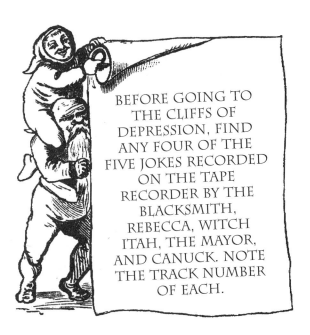

BEFORE GOING TO THE CLIFFS OF DEPRESSION, FIND ANY FOUR OF THE FIVE JOKES RECORDED ON THE TAPE RECORDER BY THE BLACKSMITH, REBECCA, WITCH ITAH, THE MAYOR, AND CANUCK. NOTE THE TRACK NUMBER OF EACH.

CLIFFS OF DEPRESSION

Take the rope from the guard rail, tie it to the tree limb, then climb down. If you *dug* up your bonding plant earlier (rather than *cut* it), it will serve as your admission to Chuckles Comedy Club. When you get the microphone, use the tape recorder to play four (*not* five) jokes. You'll win a fifth piece of the disc. Exit the club and go climb back up the cliffs. Be sure to take the rope with you when you leave. (Click on the spot where it's tied to the branch.)

10. THE LIGHTHOUSE AND BEYOND

AIR VULTURE

If you haven't done so already, use the magnet with the whistle to summon a vulture, then choose the Lighthouse. (If you've already taken a vulture ride, just click on the Lighthouse on the map.)

LIGHTHOUSE

At the door, show the keeper your illumynite. Ask him about disc pieces; he'll hand you the sixth and final piece. Go upstairs. Use the cow hitch to tie the rope to the rail. Tie the talon to the rope, then throw the rope. Climb the rope bridge to the big tree, then climb down.

BEL NAIRE TEMPLE

Take the shield from the statue. Hand the holy woman your sword. Take a vulture ride up to the Lighthouse, retrieve the rope and talon, then vulture back down to the Temple. Turn around, then take the exit that veers right out of the temple courtyard. Walk to the Dwarven Mines.

DWARVEN MINES

Put on the mining helmet. Get into the mining cart. The mine is a maze, but the correct sequence of turns can be found in the Dwarven General's speeches if you play them back on the tape recorder—left, right, straight, right, left, right, straight, right, left, left, right, straight. You'll come to the Ancient Ruins.

ANCIENT RUINS

Place the pieces of the disc in the trencher. Now you need to give one item to each statue. You can find a clue to the correct series of items and statues, from left to right, in the poem in the Mayor's files under the heading "Muses." ("Bog down not with your staff" and so on.)

Or you can cheat and give the statues (in order from left to right, excluding the *kneeling* statue in the center) the following items:

Witch's stick

Talon

Thermozz

Box and helmet (two items here)

Shield

Tele-Orb

The Flying Disc of Frobozz will be forged now if you press either button on the trencher. Take the disc. Don't forget to retrieve all the other items before you exit! Now take a vulture ride to the Troll Caverns.

11. THE TROLL CAVERNS, THE SPIDER, AND THE DAM

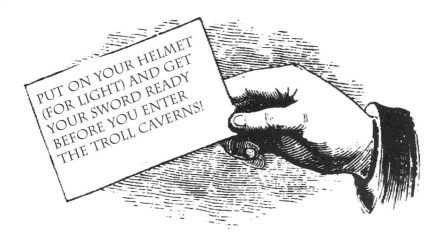

PUT ON YOUR HELMET (FOR LIGHT) AND GET YOUR SWORD READY BEFORE YOU ENTER THE TROLL CAVERNS!

TROLL CAVERNS

The skeleton's note in the sand (LUD) tells you how to defeat the three guards—left, up, down. Strike to the *left* of the first guard, swing *up* on the second guard, swing *down* on the final guard. When you meet the troll leader, threaten him repeatedly as he talks. He'll give you the Necklace of Fear. (If you let him finish his speech, you're a goner.)

FOREST OF SPIRITS

Work your way to the Giant Spider (see the map earlier). Show it the Necklace of Fear. Cut the spider web with your sword.

FLOOD CONTROL DAM 3

Remember the tile puzzle message? ("Water unseen at falls mix with bat dropping yields potion for invisibility.") Go behind the falls and fill the silver flask with water. Drop the bat guano into the flask of water to create the potion of invisibility. Now go back to the blocked path by the Cliffs of Depression.

12. ENDGAME: THE CITADEL

BLOCKED PATH

Throw the Flying Disc of Frobozz at the blocked path.

CITADEL OF ZORK

Use the bow with the arrows in your inventory, then shoot an arrow at the hand at the top of the citadel. Enter the citadel. To get past the orc leader, drink the potion of invisibility and play the recording of Alexis, the poodle from hell. Go forward to the bridge.

THE CITADEL BRIDGE

Throw inventory items at the Citadel Bridge, one by one. Finally, when the only items remaining are the map, photo album, camera, tape recorder and notebook, cross the new bridge that appears on the right.

SURVIVING MORPHIUS

Play Morphius in a game of Survivor. He's added a new rule: Whenever Morphius blocks your only move, you can "pass" —i.e., click near the screen bottom. This forces him to move. The last few moves are critical. Plan ahead!

Computer Game Books

The 11th Hour: The Official Strategy Guide	$19.95
The 7th Guest: The Official Strategy Guide	$19.95
Alone in the Dark 3: The Official Strategy Guide	$19.95
Ascendancy: The Official Strategy Guide	$19.95
Buried in Time: The Journeyman Project 2— The Official Strategy Guide	$19.95
CD-ROM Games Secrets, Volume 1	$19.95
CD-ROM Games Secrets, Volume 2	$19.99
Caesar II: The Official Strategy Guide	$19.95
Celtic Tales: Balor of the Evil Eye— The Official Strategy Guide	$19.95
Cyberia: The Official Strategy Guide	$19.95
Cyberia2: The Official Strategy Guide	$19.99
Dark Seed II: The Official Strategy Guide	$19.95
Descent: The Official Strategy Guide	$19.95
Descent II: The Official Strategy Guide	$19.99
DOOM Battlebook	$19.95
DOOM II: The Official Strategy Guide	$19.95
Hell: A Cyberpunk Thriller— The Official Strategy Guide	$19.95
Heretic: The Official Strategy Guide	$19.95
I Have No Mouth, and I Must Scream: The Official Strategy Guide	$19.95
King's Quest VII: The Unauthorized Strategy Guide	$19.95
Marathon: The Official Strategy Guide	$19.95
Master of Orion: The Official Strategy Guide	$19.95
Master of Magic: The Official Strategy Guide	$19.95
Mech Warrior 2: The Official Strategy Guide	$19.95
Microsoft Flight Simulator 5.1: The Official Strategy Guide	$19.95

To Order Books

Please send me the following items:

Quantity	Title	Unit Price	Total
_____	_____	$ _____	$ _____
_____	_____	$ _____	$ _____
_____	_____	$ _____	$ _____
_____	_____	$ _____	$ _____
_____	_____	$ _____	$ _____
_____	_____	$ _____	$ _____

Subtotal $ _____

7.25% Sales Tax (CA only) $ _____

8.25% Sales Tax (TN only) $ _____

5.0% Sales Tax (MD and IN only) $ _____

7.0% G.S.T. Canadian Orders $ _____

Shipping and Handling* $ _____

Total Order $ _____

Within Domestic U.S. *$5.00 shipping and handling charge for the first book and $.50 for each additional book.Hawaii, Foreign and all Priority Request orders: Call Order Entry department for price quote at 916/632-4400

By Telephone: With MC or Visa, call (916) 632-4400. Mon-Fri, 9-4 PST.
By Mail: Just fill out the information below and send with your remittance to:

Prima Publishing
P.O. Box 1260BK
Rocklin, CA 95677

Satisfaction unconditionally guaranteed.

My name is _____

I live at _____

City _____ State _____ Zip _____

MC/Visa#_____ Exp. _____

Signature _____